Laurence Main - The Author

Laurence Main is a full-time professional writer of footpath guides, and this is the 39th title in an impressive list. Earlier titles include:

- Arthur's Camlan, *(Street)*
- Walks in mysterious Wales, *(Sigma Press)*
- Snowdonia & North Wales, *(Bartholemew)*
- Walk Mid Wales & The Marches *(OS/Jarrold)*
- Family Walks on Anglesey *(Scarthin Books)*

Laurence was born in Oxford in 1950, on the site of a medieval priory where the 13th-century alchemist Roger Bacon had his laboratory and is buried. He has been involved in primary research into Earth Mysteries and runs regular weekend courses for those wishing to delve deeper into this fascinating subject.

He was formerly a teacher and the assistant secretary of the Vegan Society.

Married with four children, he now lives in Dinas Mawddwy, Machynlleth, Mid Wales.

In the Footsteps of King Arthur

Laurence Main

WESTERN MAIL & ECHO LTD

Acknowledgements

I would like to thank Jo Baxter, Beck Cunningham, Richie Davies, Jeff Loo, Rama Malone, Michael Morris, Julian Orbach and Letty Rowan, who were kind enough to drive me to some of the walks. Chris Barber, author of **Journey to Avalon**, was a great source of inspiration, while it was a pleasure to meet the daughter of S.G. Wildman, author of **The Black Horsemen**, whilst in Llangollen. I was honoured with a knighthood from the reincarnation of King Arthur at the summit of Carningli at Hallowe'en, 1994. Any doubts about this character were dispelled by the nature and contents of the dreams whose theme was common to all four of us on the sacred peak that night.

The countryside is continually changing. Hedges and fences are removed, footpaths are diverted and new roads created. Every care has been taken to ensure the accuracy of the route directions, however, the publishers cannot accept responsibility for changes in details given or for errors or omissions. Wet weather can affect path surfaces, making them muddy and slippery, whilst stepping stones over rivers and streams may become impassable. **The Western Mail & Echo Ltd.** would welcome details of any changes which have taken place to these routes, or of any inaccuracies.

First published in Great Britain by the Western Mail & Echo Ltd.,
Havelock Street, Cardiff CF1 1XR. 1995

Cover photograph: Tyn-y-Bwlch. View across Hafod-yr-Wyn from farmhouse ruin.

I.S.B.N. 0 9504042 4 1

Printed by Mid Wales Litho, New Inn, Pontypool, Gwent.

Contents

			Page Nº
Introduction			i
Location Map			iv
The Walks		**Distance**	
1.	Dinas Emrys	1½ miles	1
2.	Tre'r Ceiri	4 miles	9
3.	Carn March Arthur	4¼ miles	19
4.	Ty'n-y-bwlch	2 miles	27
5.	Caerleon	4½ miles	35
6.	Caerwent	3 miles	43
7.	Castell Dinas Bran	3 miles	53
8.	Llyn Llech Owain	2 miles	61
9.	Nash Point	4½ miles	69
10.	Ogmore	4 miles	77
11.	Ruthin	4½ miles	87
12.	Moel Arthur	4 miles	97
13.	Llanbadarn Fawr	4½ miles	105
14.	Cerrig Meibion Arthur	11½ miles	115
15.	Knucklas	4 miles	125
16.	Cilgerran	6½ miles	133
17.	Penbryn	4¾ miles	145
18.	Camlan	5¼ miles	155
19.	Overlooking Bardsey	1¾ miles	167
20.	Craig-y-Ddinas	6 miles	177
Walk Notes (Use these pages for your own notes)			186

Introduction

This is not another book attempting to prove who King Arthur was. Enough people have tried that. One of the most successful is Chris Barber, who comes from the Arthurian territory of Gwent. If there is one book that is an essential companion to this book of walks, it is Journey to Avalon by Chris Barber and David Pykitt (Blorenge Books, 1993). Not that this book conforms with Chris Barber's conclusions in every case (especially with the location of the Battle of Camlan). It is accepted, however, that Arthur was from South Wales and lived from the late fifth century to well into the sixth century. There really was a flesh and blood King Arthur. The object of this book is to try and follow in his footsteps.

Taking the routes in this book will lead you to places associated with King Arthur and his knights. The walks will also bring you into close contact with sacred sites and allow you to step into the world of Mother Earth, well away from television sets and motor cars. This communion with the spirit of the living planet is so essential now. Learning to respect and live in harmony with nature, before our ruthless exploitation leads to the inevitable backlash, is the task facing us today.

Long before the flesh-and-blood Arthur of the sixth century, he was the solar hero of the Celts and fought the eternal battle between good and evil, light and darkness. In a previous age he had come as Hu (pronounced He). Both Hu and Arthur dragged monsters from lakes (as at Llyn Barfog, near Route 3's Carn March Arthur). Their names have passed into the English language in the significant words of Heart and Hearth.

Taliesin described in "The Spoils of Annwn" how Arthur harrowed hell to break humanity's chains. He sailed to the Underworld in a ship of glass to free Gweir (Man) and to come back with Ceridwen's Cauldron of Inspiration and Rejuvenation (the Holy Grail). Like Osiris of Ancient Egypt, Arthur was betrayed by his sister-wife and his envious son-nephew. Ferried down-river in a funeral barge and mourned by the triple goddess the Queen of Heaven, he was expected to return.

To the Druids, the sun was a compassionate and benevolent sentient being. Souls which had gained high vibrations found rest in the sun at death, unlike the dense mass which fail to divest themselves of their earthly envelopes. Can we regard the sun as more than a chemical factory? Can we see the purpose and unity of all life? Arthur is the sun-god, the fount of our highest ideals. He dies so that others may live.

Solar energy gives life to the world. Its vibrations are absorbed and slowed down to the point of death in the process, just as 'the king must die'. Crucified on the Tree of Life, he is reborn at the winter solstice. Time allows the redemption of spirit from matter, the emergence of consciousness from sleep, the coming of new energy to defeat inertia and wisdom to conquer ignorance.

So Arthur sleeps with his knights beside a pile of gold beneath a fairy hill, awaiting the dawn of that new day when his country will need him again.

These walks will not tax the inexperienced too severely. They average four and a quarter miles in length, with the longest being an 11½ mile trek over the Preselis which includes climbing to the 1760 ft summit of Foel Cwmcerwyn. Moel Arthur attains the height of 1494 ft, Tre'r Ceiri reaches the 1400 ft mark, while the Craig-y-Ddinas and Castell Dinas Bran walks both take you above that magical 1,000ft mark, so there are some challenges.

The maps in this book are drawn at a generous scale. It is always a good idea to carry the relevant Ordnance Survey Pathfinder or Outdoor Leisure map as well, plus a good compass. Practise using them before venturing on the hills in the mist. Choose your weather (telephone for a forecast on 0839 168 369 for Snowdonia, 0839 168 385 for North Wales, 0839 168 384 for Mid and West Wales and 0839 168 379 for South Wales) and allow plenty of time to complete the walk before dusk. Carry a torch and batteries just in case you don't.

Walking boots will help you enjoy these walks, while an anorak should keep out any wind and rain. Emergency rations of food and drink can be carried in a lightweight rucksack. Refreshments are often available at the start of the walk or along the way and this information is given for each walk.

Visiting ancient sites makes a subscription to CADW (Welsh Historic Monuments) a worthwhile proposition. Full details are available from CADW, Brunel House, 2 Fitzalan Road, Cardiff, CF2 1UY (Tel. 01222 500200).

As you wander around the principality, the services of the Wales Tourist Board will prove invaluable. Contact the Wales Tourist Board at Brunel House, 2 Fitzalan Road, Cardiff, CF2 1UY (Tel. 01222 499909).

Help preserve our network of public footpaths and bridleways and enjoy them in the company of others by joining the Ramblers' Association. Contact the Ramblers' Association, Ty'r Cerddwyr, High Street, Gresford Wrexham, Clwyd, LL12 8PT (Tel. 01978 855148).

Remember the Country Code!

Enjoy the countryside and respect it.
Guard against all risk of fire.
Leave gates as you find them.
Keep your dogs under close control.
Keep to public paths across farmland.
Use gates and stiles to cross fences, hedges and walls.
Leave livestock, crops and machinery alone.
Take your litter home.
Help to keep all water clean.
Protect wildlife, plants and trees.
Take special care on country roads.
Make no unnecessary noise.

Location Map

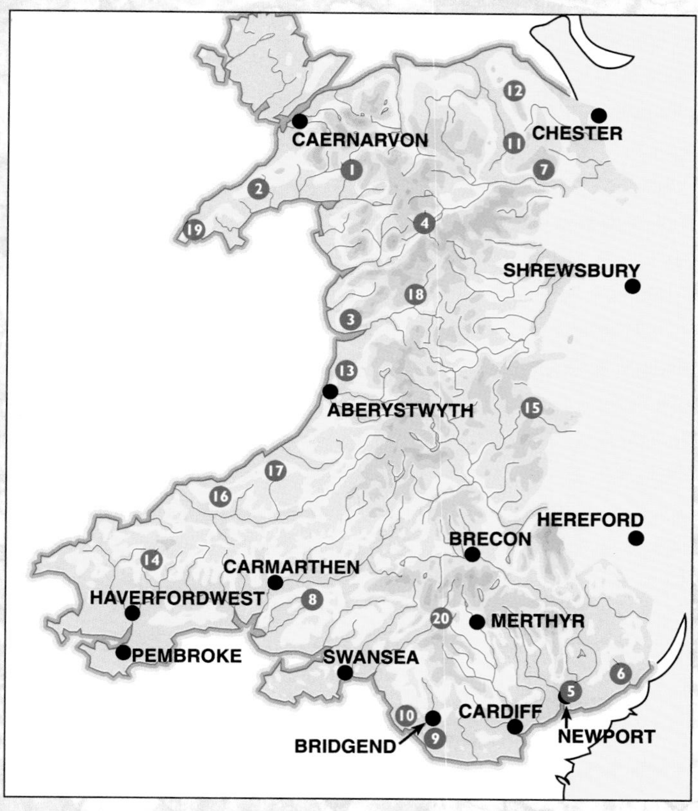

1. Dinas Emrys
2. Tre'r Ceiri
3. Carn March Arthur
4. Ty'n-y-bwlch
5. Caerleon
6. Caerwent
7. Castell Dinas Bran
8. Llyn Llech Owain
9. Nash Point
10. Ogmore
11. Ruthin
12. Moel Arthur
13. Llanbadarn Fawr
14. Cerrig Meibion Arthur
15. Knucklas
16. Cilgerran
17. Penbryn
18. Camlan
19. Overlooking Bardsey
20. Craig-y-Ddinas

KEY TO MAPS

	The footpath route
	Number corresponding with route directions
	Other paths (not always rights of way)
	Motor road
	Railway
	Hedge or fence
	River or stream with direction of flow
	Bridge
	Wall
	Buildings
	Ruin
+	Church or Chapel
G	Gate
S	Stile
P	Signpost
	Trees
	Amphitheatre, hillfort or earthwork
	Roman Walls
	Stone ring (e.g. Beddarthur)
	Standing Stones (e.g. Cerrig Meibion Arthur)
	Medieval Castle (e.g. Cilgerran)
	Cliffs (e.g. Penbryn)
N	Direction of North

Each map has a scale in miles and a gradient profile showing the height in feet above sea level and the distance in miles from the start of the walk.

Afon is Welsh for river, nant means stream

Example Map

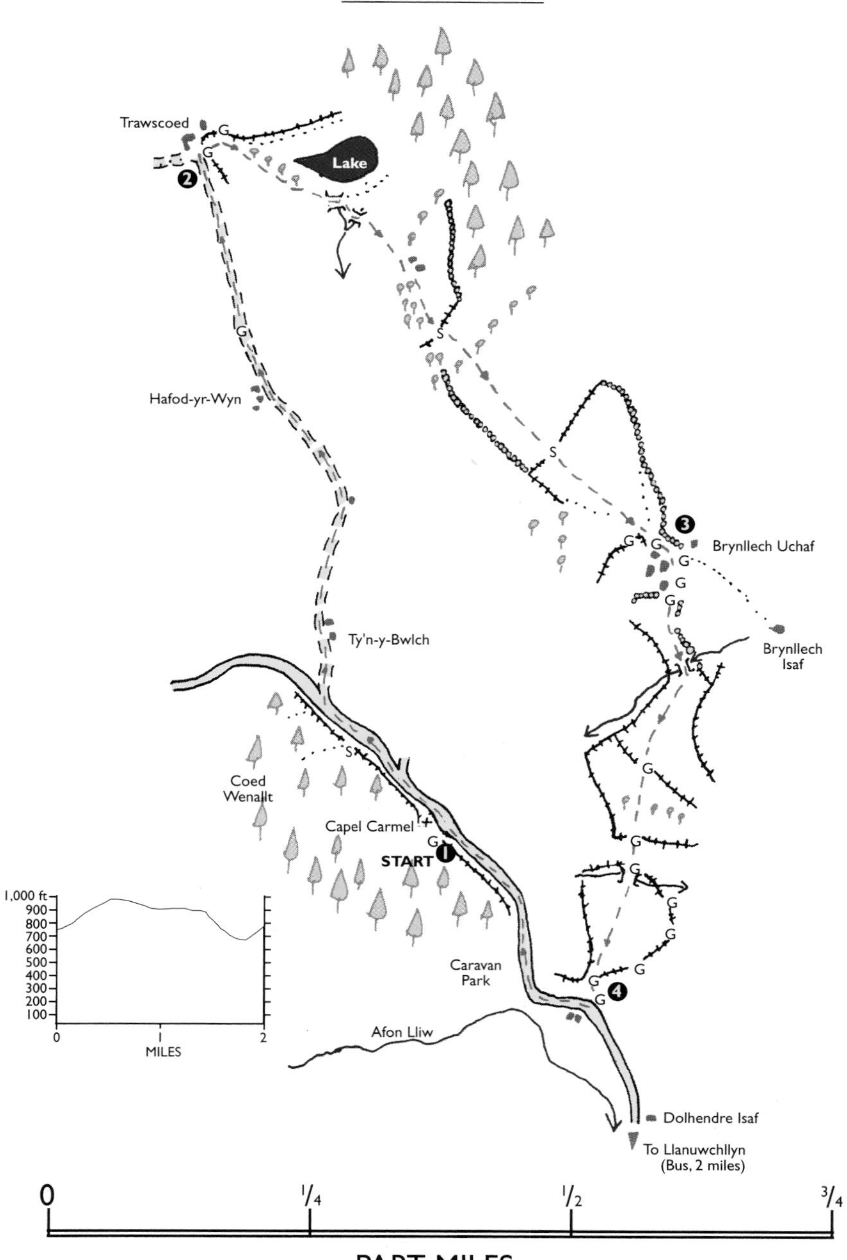

Trawscoed
Lake
Hafod-yr-Wyn
Ty'n-y-Bwlch
Brynllech Uchaf
Brynllech Isaf
Coed Wenallt
Capel Carmel
START
Caravan Park
Afon Lliw
Dolhendre Isaf
To Llanuwchllyn (Bus, 2 miles)
1,000 ft
900
800
700
600
500
400
300
200
100
0
1
2
MILES
0
1/4
1/2
3/4
PART MILES

Dinas Emrys 1

Long before the days of King Arthur, according to The Mabinogion story of Lludd and Llefelys, Lludd hid two dragons in Dinas Emrys, then called Dinas Ffaraon Dandde. In time this fortress in the heart of Snowdonia came into the hands of Vortigern, the tyrant who deceitfully gained the throne of Britain in the mid fifth century. In order to keep his crown against the opposition of the rightful heirs, who had fled to Brittany, Vortigern invited Saxon allies into the country and married Rowena, the daughter of their leader Hengist. However, the Saxons weren't content with serving the British king. They were determined to make the country their own and massacred the British chieftains who attended a peace conference. The wealthy counties of Essex, Sussex and Middlesex were soon lost to the invaders, while Vortigern's subjects threw their support behind the grandson of Magnus Maximus who was in exile in Brittany. This was Ambrosius Aurelianus, described by Gildas as the last of the Romans. Ambrosius was known as Emrys in Welsh. Emrys (Ambrosius) may also have been

Myrddin (Merlin), or at least one of the characters who gained the title of Myrddin (not to be confused with Myrddin Wyllt, Merlin the Wild, who lived in the Scottish Borders). A priest from South Wales known as Nennius compiled a history of the Britons in about 800 and recorded how Vortigern tried to build a stronghold at Dinas Ffaraon Dandde, but the walls kept collapsing. The tyrant consulted his druids, who advised the sacrifice of a boy born without a father. Such a boy was found in South Wales, where his mother denied knowing any man, implying that her son was an incubus of the devil (Myrddin was said to have a third nipple). When brought to the hillfort, he was able to show why the walls kept falling down. A pool was undermining the foundations (archaeologists have, indeed, found an artificial pool near the centre of Dinas Emrys, probably dating from the early Roman period; the most substantial remains date from the 12th century). The boy further confounded Vortigern's druids by correctly predicting the discovery of a folded tent containing two vases. One held a red dragon, while the other revealed a white one (the two dragons hidden by Lludd). They emerged to fight. The white dragon gained the advantage at first, but the red one triumphed in the end. The boy explained that the tent was Britain, the white dragon the Saxons and the red one the British. In celebration, the young Emrys (named as Myrddin Emrys by the 12th-century Geoffrey of Monmouth), claimed the citadel, telling Vortigern to flee.

Myrddin is said to have buried a treasure in a cave here, prophesying that it would be discovered one day by a blond, blue-eyed youth. The cave would open to the rightful person to the sound of bells.

Dinas Emrys

No. 2 Pathway alongside Afon Glaslyn, leading toward the A498

Distance: 1½ miles

Grid Reference: SH 607491

Maps: O.S. Outdoor Leisure 17 (Snowdonia - Snowdon area), O.S. Landranger 115 (Caernarfon & Bangor).

Parking: Lay-by beside the A498 at the start, or, if visiting the copper mine, at Sygun Copper Mine.

Public Transport: Bus no 11 (Llanberis-Beddgelert-Caernarfon) passes the start of this walk. Bus no 97 from Porthmadog (the nearest railway station) serves Beddgelert, just over one mile from the start of this route.

Refreshments: Sygun Copper Mine and in Beddgelert.

No. 3 Sygun Copper Mine

No. 4 View across Afon Glaslyn, looking toward Dinas Emrys

Start: A lay-by beside the A498 opposite Dinas Emrys. (G.R. SH 607491)

Route

1. Go left from the lay-by along the verge of the A498 road towards Beddgelert. Turn left across the bridge and up the access lane to Sygun Copper Mine.

2. Go back down the access lane but as you approach the bridge over the Afon Glaslyn turn right through a gate and along a footpath running parallel to the river, on your left. Walk upstream, initially with a wall on your left, then head for the upper of two gates ahead.

3. Go through the gate to walk with a wall and the river on your left. Eventually reach a footbridge across the river, shortly before Llyn Dinas.

4. Turn left across the footbridge and go left to walk downstream with the river on your left. Turn right with the path to cross a ladder stile beside a gate and go ahead to the A498 road.

5. Go left along the verge, passing below Dinas Emrys on your right. Reach the lay-by on your left. There is no official access up to Dinas Emrys yet, although the National Trust plan a route for 1996. Ask about it in their shop at Beddgelert.

The route map for Walk 1 - Dinas Emrys

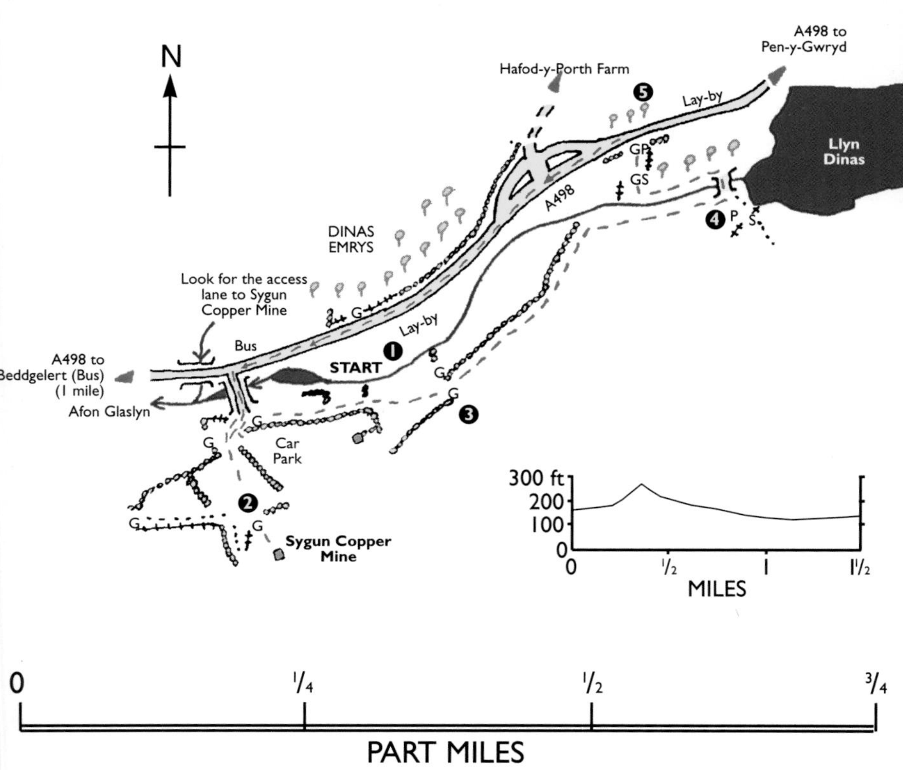

Tre'r Ceiri 2

Tre'r Ceiri (Town of the Giants) could be described as the most dramatic hillfort in Wales. It occupies the south-west summit of Yr Eifl, whose triple peaks are called The Rivals in English, although the Welsh name means The Fork. The oval site covers nearly five acres, being over 300 yards long and 100 yards wide at the furthest points. The enclosing wall is up to 15 feet thick. A parapet walk can still be seen in places and it is known that the wall was surmounted by a wooden fence. There were entrances on the north-western and southern sides. The remains of over 150 circular or oval huts have been found inside the wall, with more on levelled sites outside. The Irish may have lived here in the Bronze Age (after the giants?), but there was also a major settlement in Roman times, culminating in Vortigern's defeat around AD 465.

Vortigern moved here when Ambrosius Aurelianus returned from exile in Brittany to reclaim his inheritance from the traitor who had stolen it and was responsible for letting the Saxons into Britain. Ambrosius' army set the wooden stockade alight with fire arrows, making a spectacular beacon. Vortigern managed to slip away and find a final refuge at Little Doward Hill, on the boundary of Gwent and Herefordshire. Escaping from there, he is said to have faded away in Brittany. Ambrosius was now the leader of the Britons and he turned his attention to stemming the tide of Angles, Saxons and Jutes. The mighty earthwork known as the Wansdyke, stretching from Andover in Hampshire to Portishead in Avon,

may well have been constructed under his orders. Geoffrey of Monmouth wrote that the death of Ambrosius Aurelianus was marked by the appearance of a comet. The same comet was recorded in the Anglo Saxon Chronicle as appearing in AD 497. Ambrosius was succeeded by his brother Uther. His name was actually a title, with Uther Pendragon meaning Wonderful Head Dragon. The Roman legions marched under the emperor's purple dragon, so the Britons were maintaining Roman symbols. Uther was probably killed fighting Cerdic's Gewissei in 506. Arthur was gaining experience to take over as the chief warlord, but probably not until the rule of Geraint the son of Erbin came to an end with his death in battle at Llongborth in 508.

Tre'r Ceiri

No. 5 Entrance through north-western wall of Tre'r Ceiri

Distance:	4 miles
Grid Reference:	SH 356432
Maps:	O.S. Pathfinder 801 (Llanaelhaearn), O.S. Landranger 123 (Lleyn Peninsula).
Parking:	Park considerately in the village of Llithfaen or at a lay-by near direction point 6.
Public Transport:	Bus no 27 runs from Pwllheli (the nearest railway station) to Llithfaen. Telephone 01286 679535 for details.
Refreshments:	Llithfaen.

No. 6 Facing west with huts in foreground

No. 7 Pathway from Tre'r Ceiri down to the B4417

Start: The bus stop at the crossroads in Llithfaen. (G.R. SH 356432)

Route

1. Face the village shop and go left, eastwards, along the B4417 towards Llanaelhaearn. Reach a chapel on your right and turn left uphill along a lane which bears right.

2. Go ahead through a gate across the lane and continue along the track ahead. The 1850 ft peak of Yr Eifl is ahead on your left and the distinctive crags of Caergribin are ahead on your right. Come to a fenced bunker and pass it on your left before turning left along a moorland path.

3. Cross the ladder stile in a fence ahead and continue to go over another ladder stile to the left of a gate in a wall ahead. Go ahead up to the ruins of Tre'r Ceiri and climb to the cairn.

4. Return to the gap in the outer wall of Tre'r Ceiri and the notice board giving the hillfort's history. Descend to a fork and bear left to take the path which sweeps around the hillside, bearing left as it descends.

5. Go ahead over a ladder stile in a fence and descend with a wall on your left. Take a small metal gate in the corner ahead and keep near the wall on your left as you go downhill to reach the B4417 road.

6. Turn right along the B4417 road and follow it into Llithfaen, the start of this walk.

The route map for Walk 2 - Tre'r Ceiri

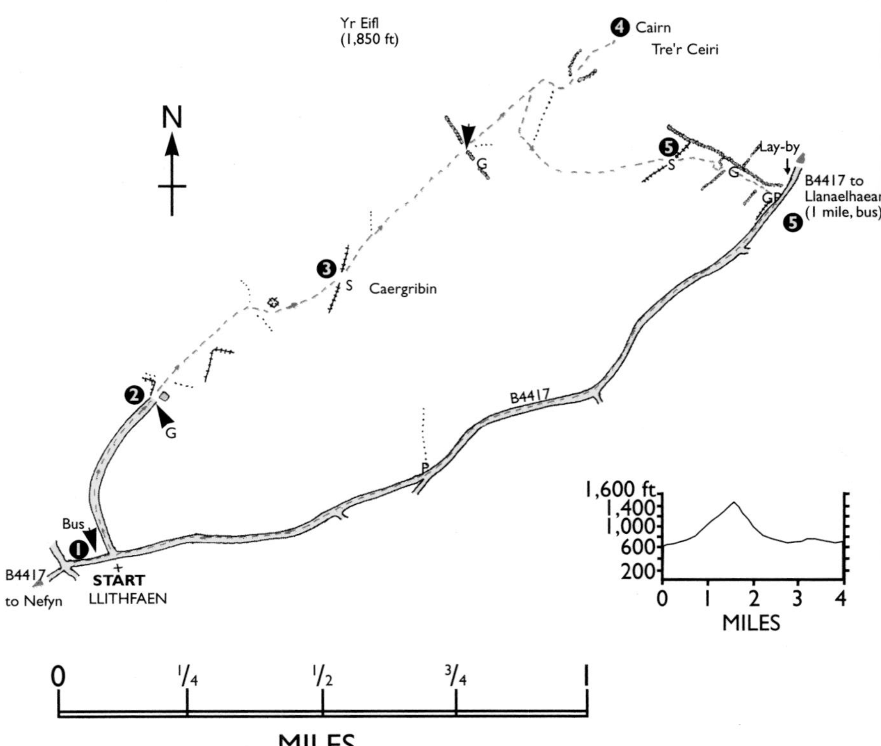

No. 8 Facing north-east from Tre'r Ceiri

Carn March Arthur 3

Arthur was the son of Meurig, the king of South Wales, the land of the Silures tribe, who also held territory in Somerset, Devon, Cornwall and Brittany. Meurig also held the title Uther Pendragon. It was the custom for Celtic chieftains to foster their sons with other rulers. Perhaps the holding of essential hostages helped to keep the peace. Arthur, who was probably born around 482, spent his early years in the company of his foster-brother Cai (the future Sir Cai) in North Wales.

Cai lived in the old Roman fortlet now known as Caer Gai (Cai's fortress) near Llanuwchllyn, Gwynedd. Spencer referred to Arthur's upbringing here in his Faery Queen:

> His dwelling is low in a valley green,
> Under the foot of Rauran mossy hole
> (Rauran is Aran, the mountain overlooking Llanuwchllyn).

Meirionnydd is where the young Arthur would have learned to ride a horse. No doubt he explored the ancient ridgeways down the Dyfi Valley towards Aberdyfi. There may well have been a fertile plain here then, being Cantre'r Gwaelod (Lowland Hundred).

Legend records how this most fertile part of

the Lord of Ceredigion's land was drowned in the sixth century. Gwyddno Garanhir was the lord and he entrusted the sea walls to Seithennin the drunkard. A storm broke them while Seithennin was wining and dining. Taliesin the bard managed to escape from the flood, as did Seithennin's sons, who atoned for their father's misdeeds by becoming saints and founding churches.

Perhaps the great flood was linked to the visit of a celestial body, recorded by contemporary astronomers in China, affecting the earth adversely and causing plagues and earthquakes around the time of much civil unrest, as with the Battle of Camlan.

Evidence of Arthur having ridden here is the rock indented with the hoofprint of Arthur's horse, Carn March Arthur. The horse is said to have carried Arthur to safety from here to the other side of the Dyfi estuary (or vice versa) when pursued by enemies. Dowsing for leys or spirit paths here does reveal a ley going to Bedd Taliesin, the grave of Taliesin, above Tre'r Ddoll. Perhaps Arthur's horse's leap is a folk memory of this ley?

Arthur is also said to have dragged a monster out of the nearby lake, Llyn Barfog, although that particular hero may well have been Hu Gadarn from around 2000 BC.

Carn March Arthur

No. 9 View from Carn March Arthur

Distance:	4¼ miles
Grid Reference:	SN 640986
Maps:	O.S. Outdoor Leisure 23 (Snowdonia - Cadair Idris area), O.S. Landranger 135 (Aberystwyth).
Parking:	There is an official Snowdonia National Park car park at the start of this walk.
Public Transport:	Trains run to Aberdyfi from Machynlleth and Pwllheli, bus no. 29 runs to Aberdyfi from Tywyn and Machynlleth. Telephone 01286 679535 for details. Walk two miles each way by road from Aberdyfi to join this route at direction no. 6.
Refreshments:	Aberdyfi.

No. 10 Look for the indented hoof print of King Arthur's horse. The slate says this is Carn March Arthur

Start: Snowdonia National Park car park in Happy Valley (Cwm Maethlon) at Tyddyn-y-briddell. (G.R. SN 640986)

Route

1. Take the gate at the back of the car park and go left along the track, away from the road. The direction is soon signposted. Bear left, then right across a stream to Tyddyn-y-briddell and turn left to pass the farmhouse on your right. Go ahead over a ladder stile beside a gate in a wall. Walk with a wall and a stream on your left. Go ahead over the next ladder stile beside a gate ahead.

2. Bear right, off the firm track, at a public footpath signpost. Go ahead to cross the stream and join the firm track again as you climb to a gate and stile beside a signpost in a higher wall. Go ahead to cross a stile to the left of a gate and continue to Llyn Barfog. Move to your right round the shore of the lake until you reach a point where you overlook a bog and can receive a good echo from a shout aimed at a cliff beyond it.

3. Retrace your steps past Llyn Barfog, now on your right. Turn left shortly after the lake and follow a path to a junction with a ridgeway track. Turn right along this, soon crossing a stile beside a gate. As you approach a wall on your left, look for the indented hoof print of King Arthur's horse in a rock on your right. A slate says this is Carn March Arthur.

4. Continue along the ridgeway, with the wall and a view over the Dyfi estuary on your left. Continue over a stile beside a gate and with a fence on your right down to a signpost just before a cottage. Take the gate to pass this cottage on your right and go ahead along a metalled lane.

5. Continue along a road, towards Aberdyfi. When the fence on your right bears right, away from the road, bear right off the road, too.

6. Descend with the rough track, going through a gate and turning right at a lower path junction. Walk with a fence on your left down to a gate giving access to woodland.

7. Descend with the track past a plantation of conifer trees and turn left with it towards a farm (Dyffryn-gwyn). Take a footbridge over a stream and pass the farm buildings on your left as you take the farm access lane to the road in Happy Valley.

8. Turn right along the road until you reach the Snowdonia National Park car park on your right.

The route map for Walk 3 - Carn March Arthur

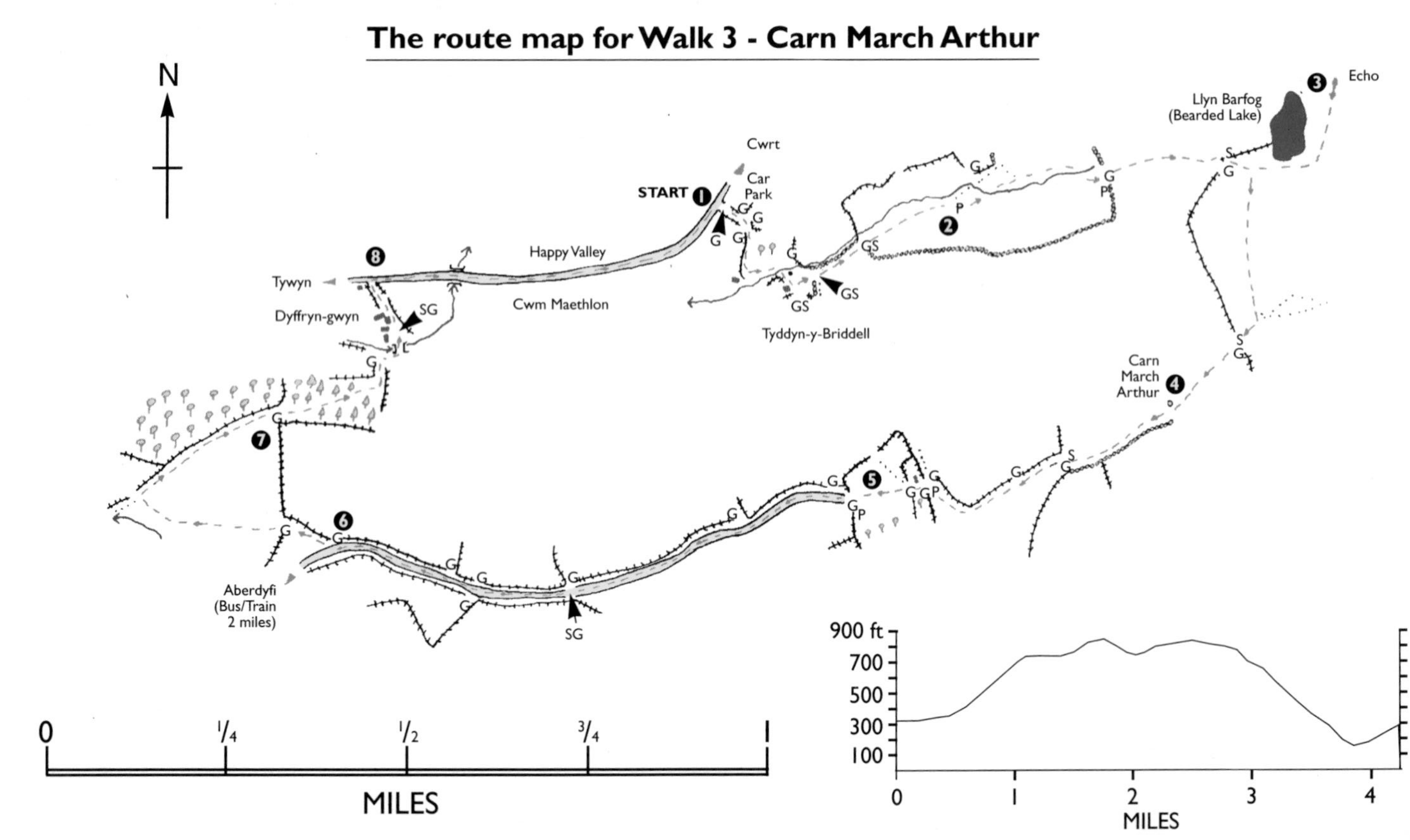

No. 11 View across Llyn Barfog

Ty'n-y-bwlch 4

The giant Rhita ruled this part of Gwynedd in Arthur's time. He waylaid travellers taking the old road over the Bwlch y Groes (SH 914228) and shaved off the beards of the chiefs he had subdued and made them into a fur cloak. He challenged Arthur to a duel, with the cloak as a prize plus the beard of the loser. Arthur, who must have been young at the time because he declared his beard wasn't very long, accepted the challenge and won, slaying Rhita.

According to Geoffrey Ashe's Guidebook to Arthurian Britain, Rhita was buried under a boulder at Ty'n-y-bwlch Farm up the valley of the Afon Lliw, to the west of Arthur's childhood home of Caer Gai. According to locals, Rhita's grave is near Tan-y-Bwlch Farm in the valley of the Afon Twrch at grid reference SH 912244.

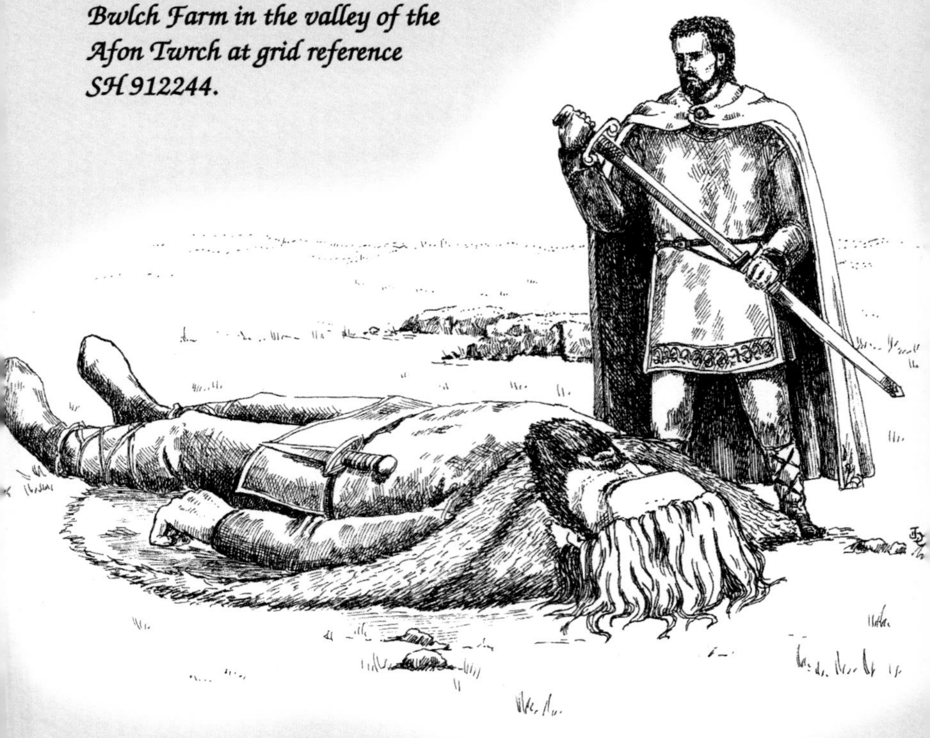

Ty'n-y-bwlch

No. 12 View across Tyn-y-bwlch

Distance:	2 miles
Grid Reference:	SH 849315
Maps:	O.S. Outdoor Leisure 18 (Snowdonia - Harlech & Bala areas), O.S. Landrangers 124 (Dolgellau) or 125 (Bala & Lake Vyrnwy).
Parking:	There is room for considerate motorists to park near Capel Carmel.
Public Transport:	Bus no 94 (Wrexham - Barmouth via Dolgellau) stops at Llanuwchllyn, two miles from the start of this walk. Telephone 01286 679535 for times.
Refreshments:	None (but Llanuwchllyn has a pub and a shop).

No. 13 Road to Trawscoed, with foxgloves in foreground

Start: Capel Carmel. (G.R. SH 849315)

Route

1. With your back to the forest of Coed Wenallt, go left up the road, soon passing Capel Carmel on your left. Ignore an access lane for Drws-cae'rgwenyn on your right, then a stile in the perimeter fence of the forest on your left. Turn right along the next access lane on your right to go past Ty'n-y-bwlch on your right, then Hafod-yr-wyn on your left and approach the buildings of Trawscoed ahead.

2. Turn right and follow a path which passes a row of trees on your left, on the other side of which is a newly-created lake. A new, wide, footbridge leads across a newly-diverted stream flowing out of this lake. Descend to cross an old footbridge over the

No. 14 View across lake, looking toward Trawscoed

original channel of this stream and head for old buildings. Trees shade an old green lane leading from these. Cross the stile ahead, above and to the left of this old green lane, when it comes to a fence. Go ahead across the next field walking parallel to a wall on your right. Cross another stile in the fence ahead and go ahead towards the buildings of Brynllech Uchaf.

3. Pass the buildings of Brynllech Uchaf on your right but leave the track which continues to Brynllech Isaf by forking right around the side of Brynllech Uchaf's buildings and going ahead through gates to emerge in a field. Descend to a footbridge and cross a stream. Continue downhill through three more gates and over another footbridge, then take a gate to gain access to the road.

4. Turn right up the road to pass a caravan park on your left before reaching Capel Carmel.

The route map for Walk 4 - Ty'n-y-bwlch

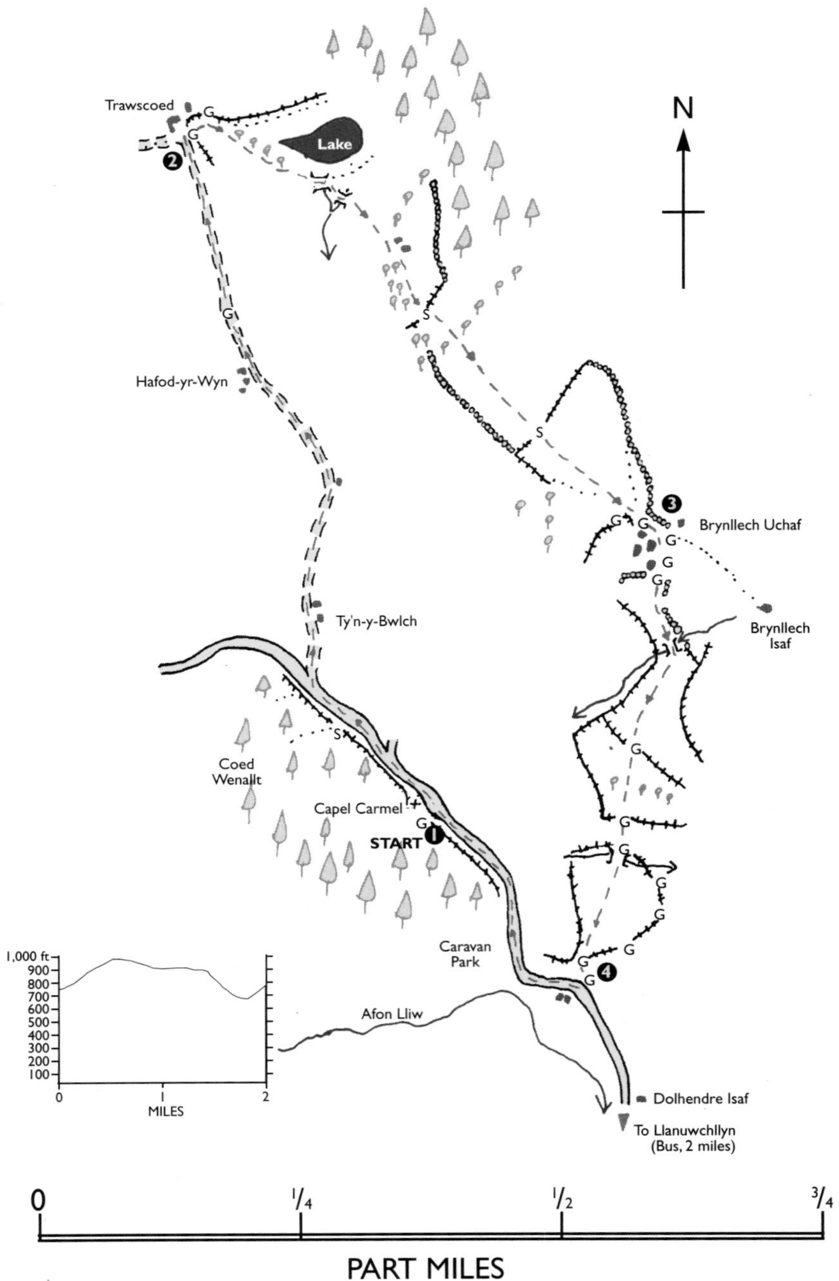

No. 15 View from farmhouse ruin

Caerleon 5

Caerleon was one of three legionary fortresses in Roman Britain, housing the Second Augusta Legion's 6,000 men. It was named Isca Silurum after the local river (Usk) and tribe (Silures). Caerleon is derived from Castra Legionum. In 1188 Giraldus Cambrensis noted in his Journey Through Wales how its "immense palaces ... once rivalled the magnificence of Rome", while it "was here that the Roman legates came to seek audience at the great Arthur's famous court". King Arthur's court was also located here by Geoffrey of Monmouth. Alfred Lord Tennyson came here in 1865 when gaining inspiration for his Idylls of the King.

The story of Peredur, son of Effrawg in The Mabinogion also states that King Arthur's court was at "Caer Llion". The Round Table was believed to be here until archaeologists dug it up to reveal a Roman amphitheatre, whose seats may have served King Arthur as a Round Table. St. Dyfrig was the Archbishop of Caerleon, although he probably crowned the young King Arthur in AD 497 across the Severn in Gloucestershire at a place called Woodchester.

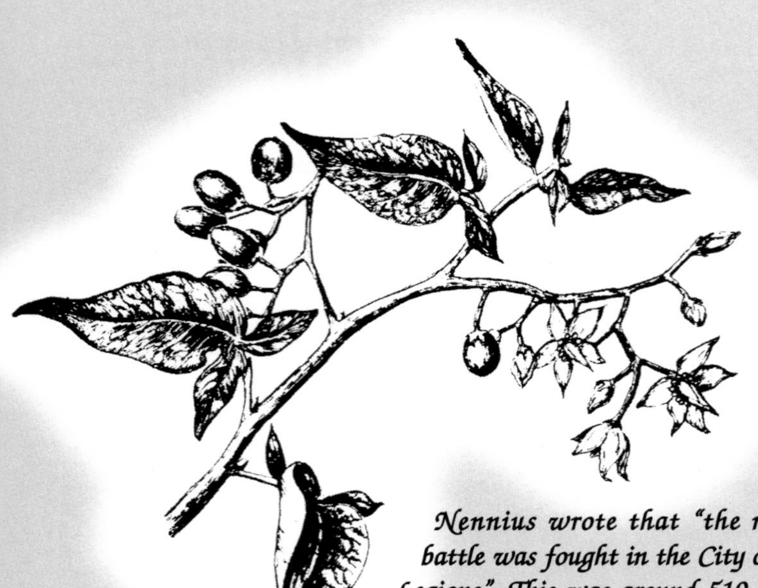

Nennius wrote that "the ninth battle was fought in the City of the Legions". This was around 510 when King Arthur was campaigning, in this case gaining the victory over the Saxons led by Osla Gyllefawr (Osla Long Knife). The battle could have taken place on the ridge above and to the east of Caerleon, with Arthur pursuing Osla towards the Severn estuary, probably along the Roman road which left Caerleon by the South Gate and crossed the Usk by a wooden bridge, leading to Cat's Ash. This place name may come from Cad Oesc, meaning the battle of Oesc, the son of Hengist, a Saxon who may have been killed at the battle.

Caerleon

No. 16 A cell within the enclosure of the amphitheatre

Distance:	4½ miles
Grid Reference:	ST 339906
Maps:	O.S. Pathfinder 1130 (Cwmbran), O.S. Landranger 171 (Cardiff & Newport).
Parking:	Near the Roman Bathhouse, Caerleon.
Public Transport:	Bus no 7/7B runs to Caerleon from Newport and Cwmbran. Telephone 01633 832478 for details.
Refreshments:	Pubs and shops in Caerleon.

No. 17 View across Great Bulmore

Start: Roman Legionary Museum, Caerleon. (G.R. ST 339906)

Route

1. With your back to the Roman Legionary Museum, go over the crossroads and down the lane giving access to the Roman amphitheatre, on your left. Turn left over a stile to follow the signposted path past the amphitheatre, now on your right. Reach the end of a wall on your left and bear left over a stile to cross a field diagonally and emerge over another stile at a road junction. Turn right to walk with the River Usk on your left, then turn left with the road to take the bridge over the Usk.

2. Keep straight on, ignoring a road that forks right. Turn left along Lulworth Road and bear right with Isca Road, walking with the river on your left. Reach a T junction where you face the Bell Inn and go left along a lane.

3. Bear right over a stile and along a signposted and waymarked path which climbs a hillside rich in blackberries at the end of summer. Go ahead over two waymarked stiles, then turn right to climb steeply to a stile in the top right hand corner of a slope planted with young trees. Cross this stile to reach a golf course.

4. Turn left to keep clear of the golf links and, later, a reservoir, whilst enjoying the view across the Usk Valley to Caerleon on your left. When you reach a corner, turn right to walk with a hedge on your left to a stile in the corner ahead which you cross to join a road believed to date back to Roman times. Go left along this road and pass Catsash House on your left.

5. Turn left at a signpost to follow a firm track until it bends left. Go ahead at this corner over a waymarked stile and continue downhill over five more stiles, gaining views across the Usk Valley and reaching the lane at Great Bulmore.

6. Turn left along the lane back into Caerleon, where the Roman Bathhouse can be visited.

No. 18 The Amphitheatre.
This may have served King Arthur as a Round Table

No. 19 Sunset on the Usk River from Great Bulmore

The route map for Walk 5 - Caerleon

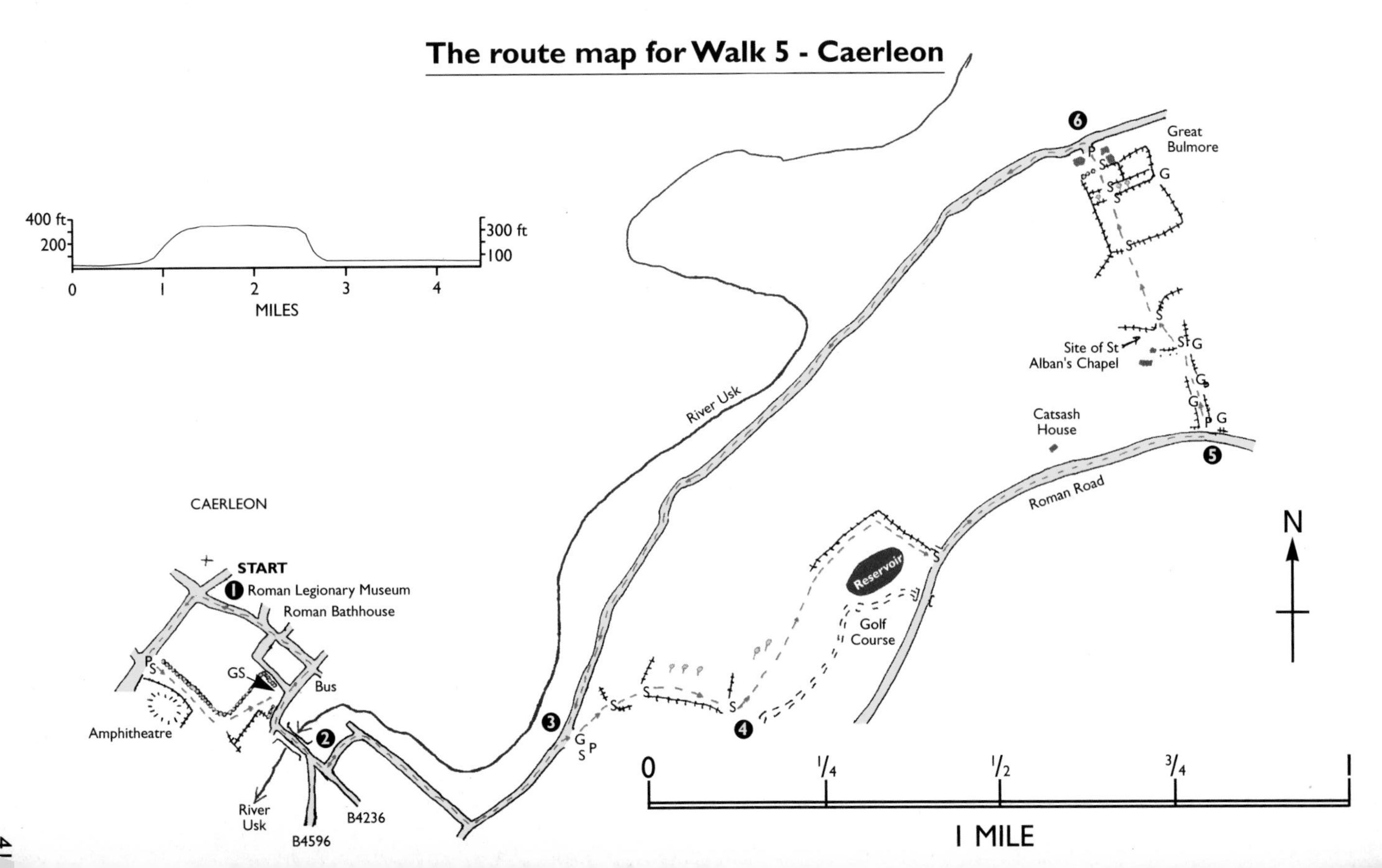

Caerwent 6

The imposing ruins of Caerleon may not have been Arthur's Camelot. Whereas Caerleon was a Roman city, Caerwent was the tribal town of the Silures. Known as Venta Silurum, it replaced the tribe's former settlement a little to the north at Llan-melin hillfort. Both Caerwent and Llan-melin hillfort must be considered as candidates for Arthur's Camelot.

The Silures were the most worthy opponents the Romans encountered in Britain. A branch of the Veneti tribe from what is now Brittany, their kings continued to rule within the Roman Empire, much as British India worked with local rulers. When the

Romans withdrew, the Silures were well able to look after themselves.

After about 1800 years, the Roman walls of Caerwent still stand impressively enclosing nearly 20 hectares. The Silures were enticed from their wattle and daub huts on Llan-melin hillfort by Caerwent's sophisticated shops, baths, town hall, amphitheatre and other buildings.

St Tathan built a church and a college at Caerwent but the Silures seem to have preferred to return to their hillfort at Llan-melin when Saxon invaders threatened. Llan-melin may well have been the Gelliwig in Cernyw that the Welsh Triads mention as one of Arthur's "Three Principal Courts in the Island of Britain". Cernyw was here in South Wales. Cornwall wasn't called Cernyw until the 10th century. Arthur's Cernyw was the coastal strip between Chepstow and Cardiff.

King Arthur used to celebrate Christmas, Easter and Whitsun at Gelliwig, where Bedwin was bishop. Bedwin Sands lie in the Severn estuary south of Caerwent. Llan-melin used to be known as Llan y Gelli (the church of the grove). This is the Gelliwig in Cernyw to which Arthur withdrew to recuperate after dealing with the Twrch Trwyth, as related in the story of Culhwch and Olwen in The Mabinogion.

Caerwent

No. 20 Perspective of the south wall

Distance:	3 miles
Grid Reference:	ST 468906
Maps:	O.S. Pathfinder 1131 (Chepstow) and 1150 (Mid Severn Estuary), O.S. Landranger 171 (Cardiff & Newport).
Parking:	Near the entrance to the church in Caerwent.
Public Transport:	Bus no 73 stops in Caerwent on its way between Newport, Chepstow and Gloucester. Telephone 01633 832478 for details.
Refreshments:	Shop in Caerwent.

No. 21 The walls of Caerwent surrounding St Stephen's Church

No. 22 Steps at West Wall

Start: St Stephen's Church, Caerwent. (G.R. ST 468906)

Route

1. Go through the gate into the churchyard and bear left, as signposted to pass the church on your right. Leave the churchyard by a stone stile in the corner and turn right along an enclosed path to reach the old Roman walls. Turn left to walk with the Roman walls to a road.

2. Go right along the pavement of the road, passing Canon Lane on your left, a stile on your right and two signposted paths plus a road on your left. Climb to pass the access lane to Brockwells Farm on your right, then turn right along a quiet lane. Ignore a signposted path going over a stile into a golf course ahead. Bear right with the lane, then left.

3. Turn right over a stile beside a gate to follow the signposted path over a stile at the far end of this field and downhill through gates. Turn left to cross a cattle grid.

4. Go right with a track and almost immediately turn right across a footbridge and over a stile. Go ahead through a field and bear left to cross a stile in its far fence. Turn left over another stile in the fence on your left and cut across the corner on your right to go over another stile. Follow the waymarked route over the next fence to reach the road by a stone stile next to a signpost.

5. Go right along the road and soon turn right over a stone stile to walk along the top of the Roman walls to where you first joined them. Retrace your steps from here by going left back to the church. The hillfort of Llan-melin is at grid reference ST 461926 but there is no official access to it.

No. 23 The impressive scale of Caerwent. These walls still stand, enclosing nearly 20 hectares

No. 24 West Wall

The route map for Walk 6 - Caerwent

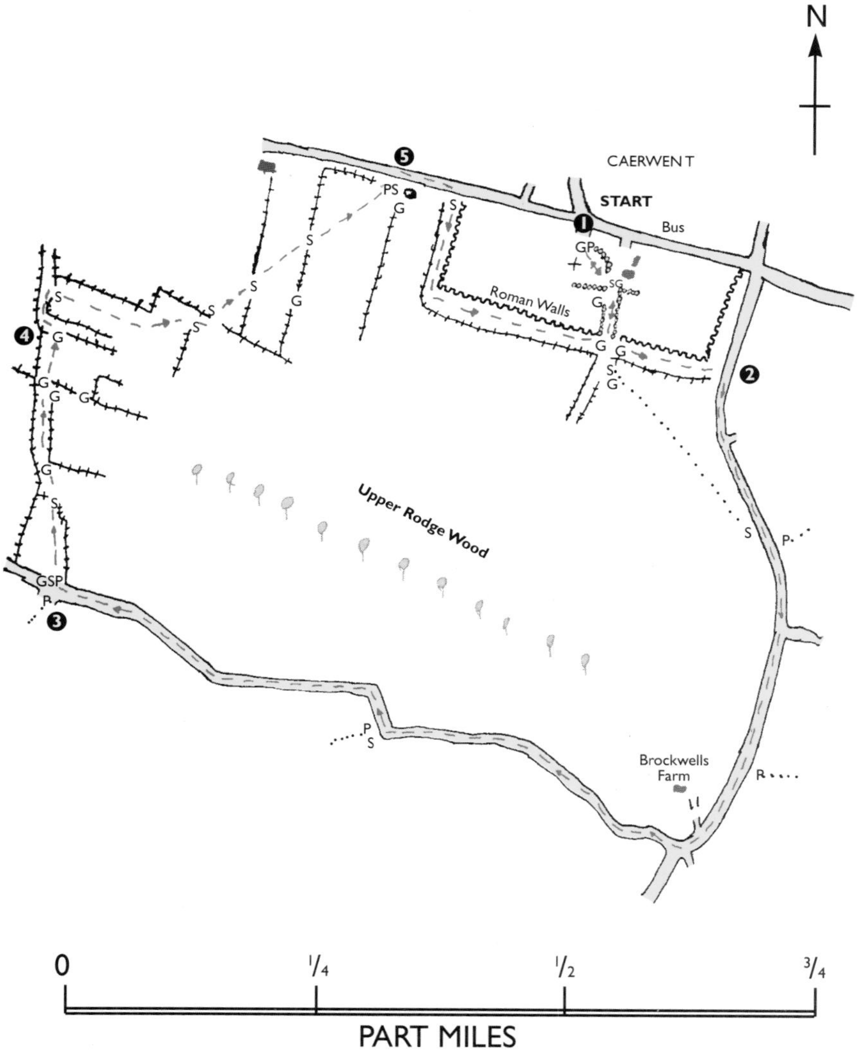

N

CAERWENT
START
Bus
Roman Walls
Upper Rodge Wood
Brockwells Farm

0 1/4 1/2 3/4
PART MILES

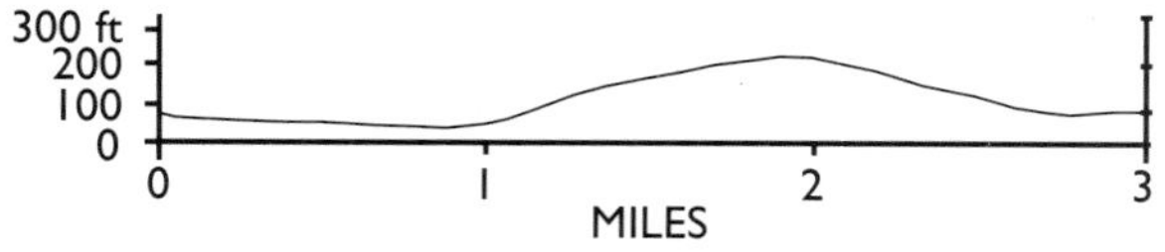

300 ft
200
100
0
0 1 2 3
MILES

Castell Dinas Bran 7

This is the Welsh version of Glastonbury Tor - indeed it is strange to note that St Collen is linked with both Llangollen and Glastonbury. At over 1000 feet, Castell Dinas Bran is twice the height of the Tor. It has Iron Age ramparts and the ruins of a mediaeval castle plus the legend of a golden harp that can only be found by a boy with a white dog which has a silver eye. This could be the mystical Arthur's Castle of the Grail. Its name refers to Bran the Blessed, the hero of a tale in The Mabinogion. Dinas Bran is mentioned in Perlesvaus or The High History of the Holy Grail. The old French name for the Castle of the Grail was Corbenic, which is derived from corbin, meaning raven or crow. Another meaning of Castell Dinas Bran is Crow Castle. The holy grail may be the union of the earth's male and female energies at this point. Dowsing can reveal female energy forming a cup shape around this hill's summit. Male energy can be dowsed penetrating this.

Castell Dinas Bran

No. 25 View of Llangollen through castle wall

Distance:	3 miles
Grid Reference:	SJ 215 420
Maps:	O.S. Pathfinder 806 (Llangollen & Wrexham South), O.S. Landranger 117 (Chester).
Public Transport:	Buses serving Llangollen include the no 94 (Wrexham - Dolgellau - Barmouth). Telephone 01352 704035 for details.
Refreshments:	Llangollen has a choice of places.

No. 26 The dramatic ruins of Castle Dinas Bran

Start: Tourist Information Centre, Llangollen. (G.R. SJ 215420)

Route

1. With your back to the Tourist Information Centre, go left down Castle Street to cross Llangollen Bridge. Turn right on its other side and take a road on your left to climb up to the Llangollen Canal. Cross this by a bridge.

2. Go ahead up a signposted public footpath, passing a school on your left. Emerge at a path junction where, ignoring the private track to Geufron on your right, you go ahead, as signposted for Castell Dinas Bran. Walk up the right-hand edge of this parkland and continue through a gate in the corner ahead. Go ahead at the next crosstracks, as signposted for Castell Dinas Bran.

No. 27 Footpath up-hill to Castle Dinas Bran. Summit 1,062 ft.

3. Emerge at the foot of the hill bearing Bran's Castle and follow the waymarked path which winds its way up to its summit, initially forking right. Descend on its far side, with Trevor Rocks in front of you. Approach a stile giving access to a lane near a corner with a fence on your right but do not cross it. Turn left to walk parallel to the lane on your right until a second stile giving access to the lane.

4. Turn left, away from the stile and follow the path around the foot of Castell Dinas Bran on your left to rejoin your outward path and retrace your steps into Llangollen.

The route map for Walk 7 - Castell Dinas Bran

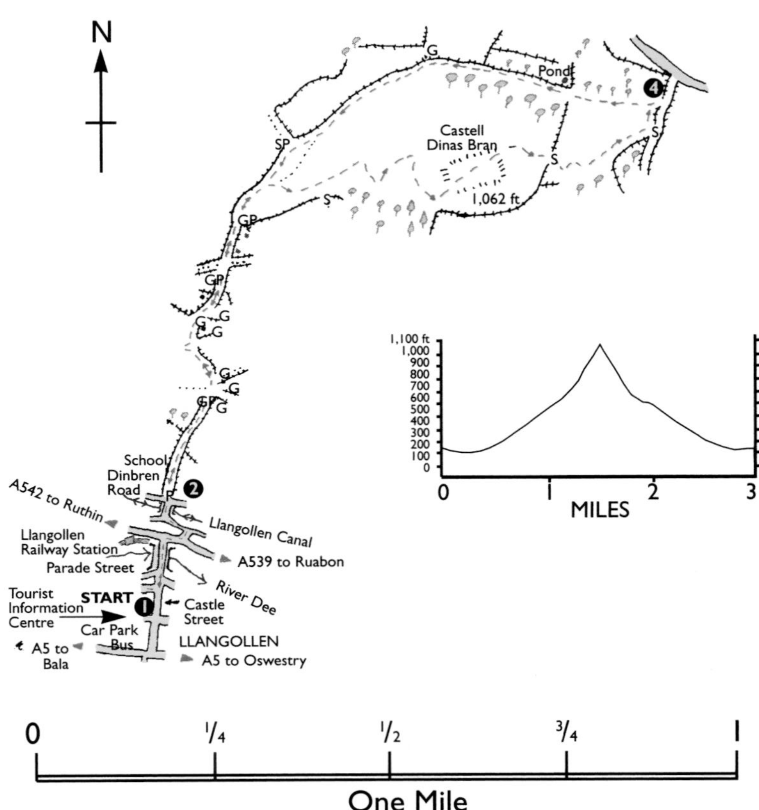

No. 28 River Dee in Llangollen

Llyn Llech Owain 8

This lake was formed by accident when Sir Owain, one of King Arthur's knights, rested here and forgot to replace the stone lid covering a spring. The spring had been given to local shepherds by the fairies so that they and their sheep could quench their thirst at this altitude. The spring had a stone lid which the fairies told the shepherds must be replaced. Not knowing this, Sir Owain had uncovered the spring when he rode this way, allowing his horse and himself a long drink. He then slept, only to wake up to find the land around him was covered by water. The knight only prevented it from growing deeper and flooding elsewhere by jumping on his horse and galloping three times around the newly-formed lake. Legend says that Sir Owain and his men still sleep in a cave at nearby Carmel Woods (SN 591 162). Some say this cave is the last resting place of Owain Lawgoch (Owain of the Red Hand), a grandson of Rhodri, a younger brother of Llywelyn the Last. He became an ally of the French and hurt his hand when attempting to capture Guernsey for France in 1372. This Owain was murdered by John Lambe in France, however, suggesting that the cave and its legend is more suitably associated with King Arthur's Sir Owain. A dowser, Elizabeth Sulivan, has pinpointed where his bones may be found, where Alfred McAlpine intend to quarry.

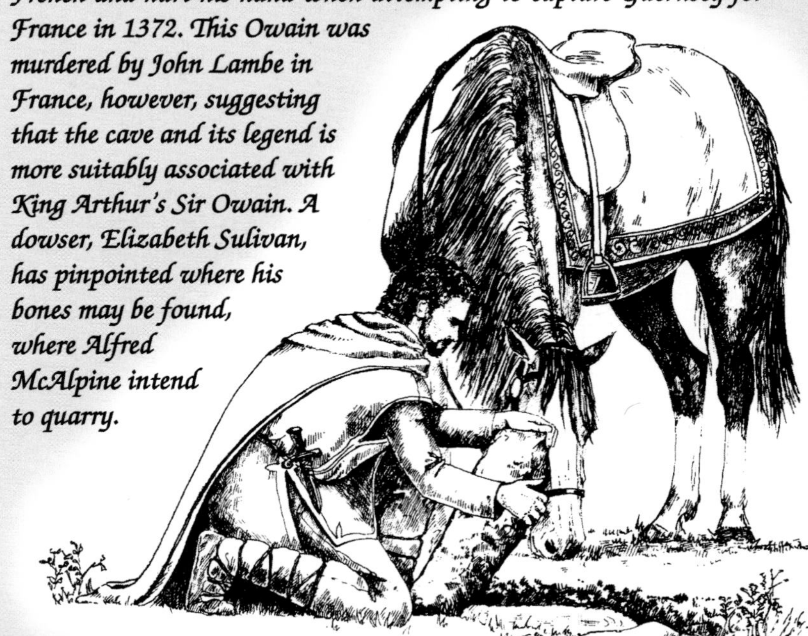

Llyn Llech Owain

No. 29 Pathway through woodland surrounding Llyn Llech Owain

Distance:	2 miles
Grid Reference:	SN 565148
Maps:	O.S. Pathfinder 1082 (Cross Hands & Pontyberem), O.S. Landranger 159 (Swansea & The Gower)
Parking:	There is a car park in the Llyn Llech Owain Country Park at the start of this walk.
Public Transport:	Telephone 01267 231817 for details of buses to Gorslas.
Refreshments:	At the Visitor Centre, Llyn Llech Owain Country Park and at Gorslas.

Start: Car Park in Llyn Llech Owain Country Park, near Gorslas. (G.R. SN 565148)

Route

1. Start by taking the signposted walk from the back of the car park, where there is a stile. Almost immediately, turn left along a path which has been constructed over the bog. You are warned not to step off this path! Cross a footbridge over a stream and bear right to reach the lake, Llyn Llech Owain, ignoring a path coming over another footbridge on your right. Reach the Visitor Centre.

2. Pass below the Visitor Centre on your left and above the lake on your right. Go under an arch and climb to a track on your left. Turn right along this track into the forest. Ignore turnings to your left.

3. Turn right with the firm forest track and follow it until you come to a fence and open countryside ahead.

No. 30 Wetland at the edge of the lake. Llyn Llech Owain supports both dragonflies and newts

4. Turn right with the forest track to walk between conifer trees on your right and the perimeter fence on your left. Turn left with the track at a corner where a path on your right provides a diversion back to the lake.

5. Follow the firm track as it turns right through forest land, some of which has been cleared or was left unplanted, then with trees on your right and the perimeter fence on your left again.

6. Bear right with the track into the forest and soon follow a bend on your left. Ignore a path on your left to bear right and emerge back in the car park.

No. 31 Foxgloves grow in abundance in the bogland

The route map for Walk 8 - Llyn Llech Owain

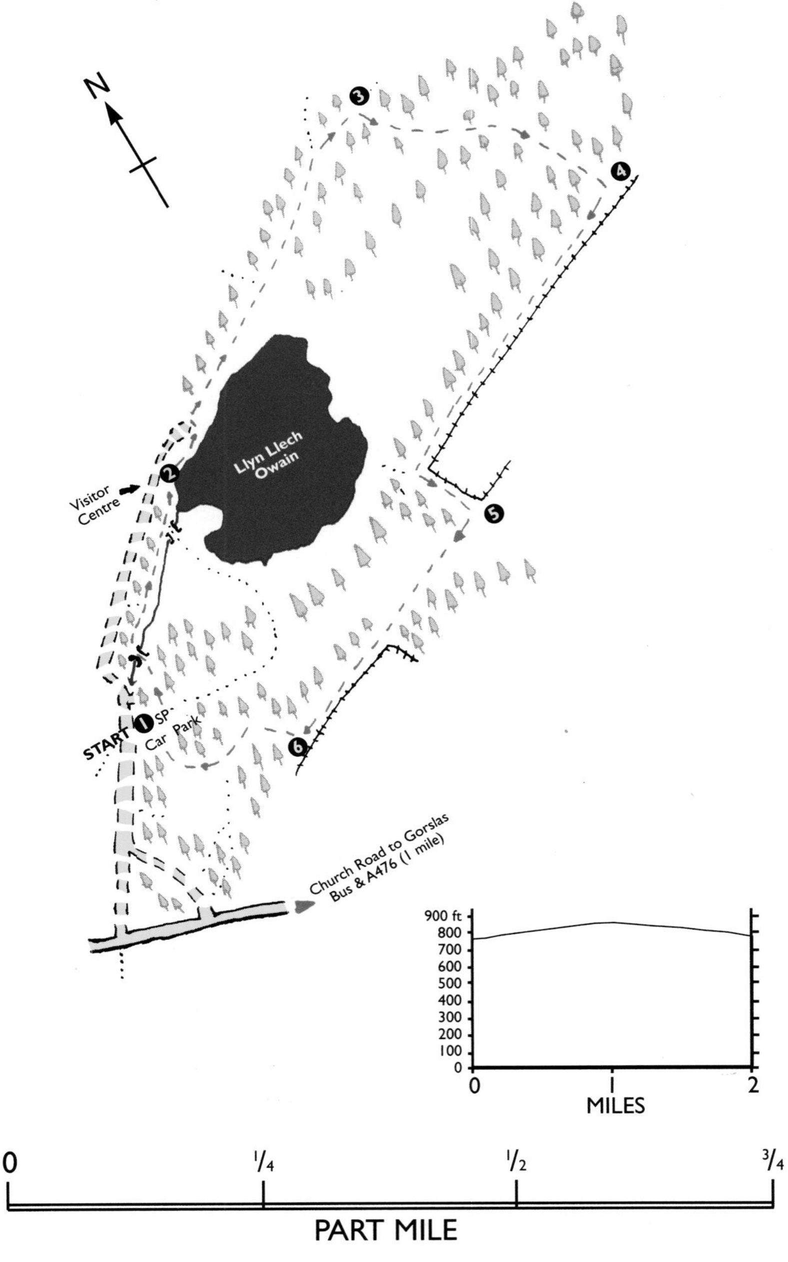

No. 32 View of the Visitor Centre across Llyn Llech Owain

Nash Point 9

This walk takes you along the Glamorgan Heritage Coastal Path, affording views of the strata that distinguish these cliffs, the Bristol Channel and of Somerset and Devon. This was the southern edge of King Arthur's homeland and two of the coastal fortifications intended to secure its defence are seen from this walk, on the northern side of Nash Point and at St. Donat's. Clifftop forts here guarded potential landing places and provided an early warning system for the Vale of Glamorgan. The central fortress was at Pentre Meurig, named after King Arthur's father. The perpetual choir and Celtic Christian university at Llantwit Major was nearby.

Caractacus had moved here in the first century, when Britain lost her independence to Rome but gained the pure Way of Jesus from contact with the young Jesus, his great-uncle Joseph of Arimathea and the early Christians who sheltered in Caractus' palace of exile in Rome. His daughter met St. Paul in Rome before returning here. St. Donat's Church is certainly

very old, although it was known as St. Gwerydd's before the coming of the Normans. Ceri was the local ruler in Caractacus' day and he fought bravely against Rome. His grave is near the start of this walk, at the site of the old church. St. Donat's Castle was bought by the American press baron William Randolph Hearst in 1925. Since 1962 it has accommodated the students of Atlantic College.

The most tangible link with King Arthur in South Wales is the Samson Stone housed in St. Illtud's Church in nearby Llantwit Major. This refers to Artmal or Arthmael – Arthur. St. Samson was King Arthur's nephew, being the elder son of his sister Anna of Gwent. The inscription refers to Arthur's very last battle, fought in Brittany, where he died, as St. Armel.

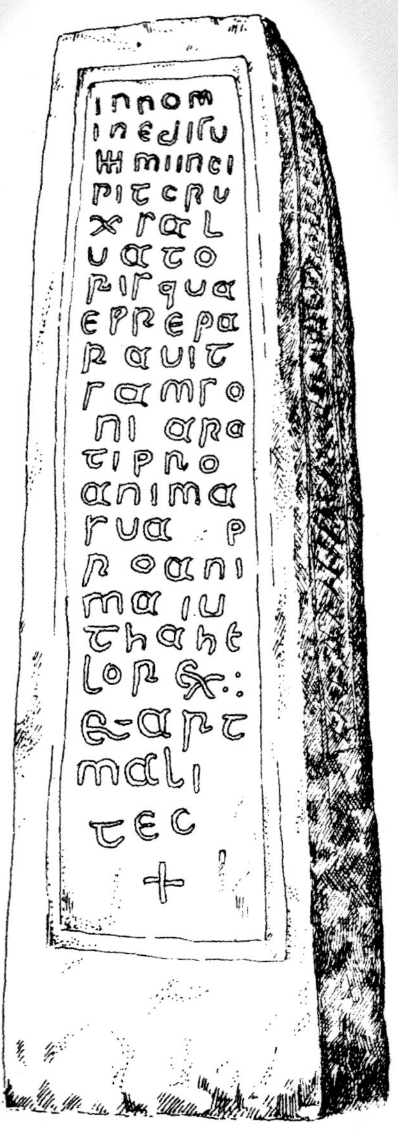

Nash Point

No. 33 Nash Point

Distance: $4^1/_2$ miles

Grid Reference: SS 916684

Maps: O.S. Pathfinder 1163 (Bridgend South & Porthcawl), O.S. Landranger 170 (Vale of Glamorgan & Rhondda areas).

Parking: There is a car park at the start of the walk, at Nash Point.

Public Transport: Bus no 145 (Cardiff-Llantwit Major-Bridgend) serves St. Donat's. Telephone 01222 873252 for details.

Refreshments: Bring your own! There may be a seasonal ice cream van at Nash Point. Refreshments are available in nearby Llantwit Major. There is a pub in Marcross.

No. 34 The Glamorgan Heritage Coast, as seen from the site of the cliff-top fort

No. 35 The beach at Nash Point

Start: Nash Point car park. (G.R. SS 916684)

Route

1. Go towards the sea from the car park and bear left to walk with the sea on your right and the site of the extremely ancient church (where Ceri was buried in the first century) on your left. Join the access lane to Nash Lighthouse and continue past this beacon on your left.

2. Go ahead over a stile and follow the clifftop path, keeping the sea on your right. Go down steps and through trees, then pass Atlantic College on your left. Go ahead with a fence on your left and cross a stile near a junction with an inland path.

3. Turn inland along the path which keeps close to a wall on your left. Emerge through a gate in the corner ahead onto a road and go left to a bus stop at the entrance to Atlantic College. Fork right along the main road.

4. Turn left down the next access lane to Atlantic College. Pass St. Donat's Castle on your left and go ahead to visit the old church at St. Donat's.

5. Retrace your steps a few paces and bear left across a bridge and follow this track up to a road. Go left along the road to its junction with the main road.

6. Turn left along the main road and reach the crossroads at Marcross. Turn left here along the access lane for Nash Point.

7. Turn right to descend into a valley and cross a footbridge. Turn left and walk downstream. Emerge from the woodland and follow the path across the stream five times before bearing left up to the car park at Nash Point.

The route map for Walk 9 - Nash Point

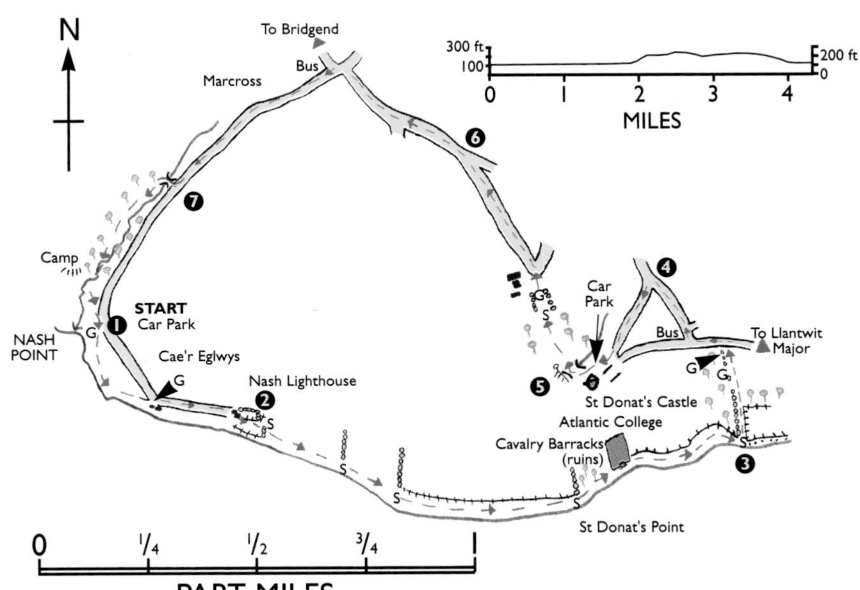

Ogmore 10

Important evidence for King Arthur's existence in South Wales was found by accident at Ogmore Castle. The Arthmail stone was used as a paving stone in the castle before its discovery and removal to the National Museum of Wales. It states:

> *"Be it known to all that Arthmail (Arthur) has given this field to God, to Glywys and to Nertart and to Bishop Fili."*

Glywys was the brother of St Cadoc, Arthur's cousin. The old name for Merthyr Mawr was Merthyr Glweis or Glwys and Glywys is probably buried in the church there. Nertart may well have been Nyvein, one of the many daughters of Brychan, another of Arthur's cousins. Bishop Fili was the person whom Caerphilly is named after and he was the son of St Cenydd.

This and the Samson Stone kept in the church at Llantwit Major are convincing proof that King Arthur really did hail from South Wales. Arthur was able to grant this land. Perhaps Glywys and Nertart were married to each other, with Bishop Fili being their spiritual adviser.

Ogmore

No. 36 Stepping stones across the Ewenny River at Ogmore Castle

Distance:	4 miles
Grid Reference:	SS 882769
Maps:	O.S. Pathfinder 1163 (Bridgend South and Porthcawl), O.S. Landranger 170. (Glamorgan and Rhondda area)
Parking:	There is a car park at Ogmore Castle.
Public Transport:	Bus No. 145 (Cardiff - Llantwit Major - Bridgend) stops at the bus shelter near the start of this walk. Telephone 01222 873252 for details.
Refreshments:	There is a pub near the start of this walk.

No. 37 The ruins of Ogmore Castle

Start: Ogmore Castle (G.R. SS 882769)

Route

1. There are two ways to cross the Ewenny River from Ogmore Castle. Stepping stones provide an exciting passage immediately from the castle ruins. When the water level is high, however, it may be safer to go around by the footbridge a short distance upstream. If possible, go out one way and back by the other. So, EITHER take the stepping-stones across the Ewenny River from Ogmore Castle and follow the walled path which bears right to the suspension bridge across the Ogmore River, OR go left from the castle ruins up the access lane to the B4524 road. Turn left along its pavement and reach a bus shelter on your

No. 38 Horses drinking at Ewenny River

left. Turn left through the kissing-gate immediately after this and follow an enclosed path to a footbridge. Cross this and bear slightly left through a meadow to go over a stile at the right-hand end of a wall ahead, near the suspension bridge across the Ogmore River on your right. Cross the suspension bridge.

2. Follow the lane to a T junction and fork left to pass St Teilo's Church, Merthyr Mawr, on your right. Continue along the lane to pass Ton Fruit Farm.

3. Immediately after Ton Fruit Farm, bear right over a stone stile in the wall and go ahead up the right-hand edge of a field. Pass a walled patch of woodland on your right as you go ahead over a stile in the wall ahead. Bear slightly left as you continue down the hill to a gate in the wall facing you in the bottom of the valley.

4. Take the gate in the wall and go ahead with a path which merges with a track coming from your left and turns right towards Candleston Farm. Fork left in the farmyard to follow a walled path which bends right and then left to emerge through a gate in the corner of a field with woodland behind the wall on your right.

5. Turn right and notice a gate in the wall on your right giving access to the woodland. Go ahead with the wall on your right, passing firstly a wooden ladder stile allowing access out of the wood on your right, then, just before a gate in the corner ahead, a metal ladder stile also leading from Coed Cwintin. Go ahead along the right-hand edge of the next field to another gate. Go through it and bear right, but leave the perimeter wall of the woodland as it makes a right turn. Cross pasture to a gap in a line of trees marking an old, broken, wall. Go through to the next field.

No. 36 Cottage on the Village green

6. Turn right to return through another gap in the old broken wall marked by a line of trees. Walk down the left-hand edge of the field to where a broken stile shows where to cross the fence in the corner, near the perimeter wall of the woodland ahead. Bear left to a gap in the hedge on your left near the corner of the next field. Ford a stream and turn right through a gate into another field. Keep to the right-hand edge of this as you climb to pass Whitney Farm on your left and follow its access track to the corner of a lane.

7. Go right down the lane back to Merthyr Mawr and return across the suspension bridge over the Ogmore River. Either take the path back over the stepping stones or the footbridge to reach the ruins of Ogmore Castle.

No. 37 St Teilo's Church

No. 38 Early Christian stone carvings at St. Teilo's church

The route map for Walk 10 - Ogmore

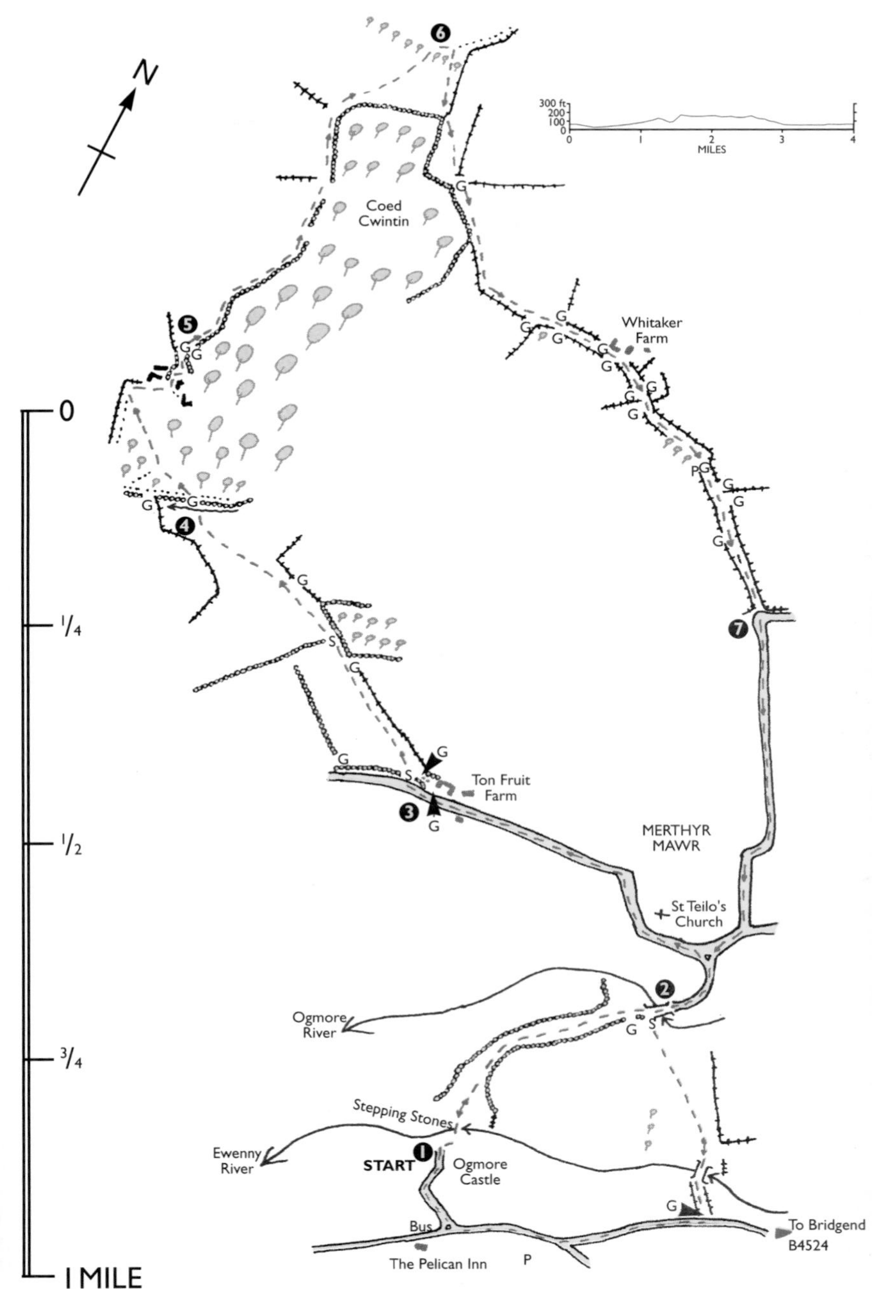

Ruthin 11

The return leg of this walk, past Ty'n-y-caeau, follows the course of an old Roman road (from St Asaph to Corwen?), which may have been used by King Arthur. We know that he did come this way. We know so little about his life because of what happened here. Maen Huail, the block of stone at the start of this walk, earned its name when Huail the son of Caw was beheaded on it by King Arthur. Huail was the ruler of Edeirnion in North Wales and a brother of Gildas, the historian who wrote De Excidio Britanniae (On the Destruction of Britain). Huail had been an enemy of Arthur, but his death so annoyed Gildas that he threw all the books he had written about King Arthur into the sea, thus opening the door to countless writers speculating on the true story of Arthur. One colourful account of the beheading is that Huail and Arthur were rivals in love for a certain lady. They fought and Huail wounded Arthur in the knee. Arthur agreed to forgive Huail on condition that the wound wasn't to be mentioned. Soon afterwards, Arthur disguised himself as a woman and went to a dance at Ruthin where his mistress was also. Huail realised that the "woman" was the disguised Arthur because of his limp and remarked that "she" would be a fine dancer if it wasn't for "her" lame knee. This remark released Arthur from his obligation and led to Huail's beheading.

Ruthin

No. 42 Maen Huail Stone

Distance: 4½ miles

Grid Reference: SJ 124583

Maps: O.S. Pathfinders 772 (Denbigh) and 788 (Ruthin), O.S. Landranger 116 (Denbigh and Colwyn Bay).

Parking: There are car parks in Ruthin.

Public Transport: Buses that stop in Ruthin include No. 51, running between Rhyl and Corwen via Denbigh. Telephone 01352 704035 for details.

Refreshments: Pubs and shops in Ruthin and Rhewl.

No. 43 Path to River Clywedog

Start: Maen Huail, the stone outside Barclay's Bank in St Peter's Square, Ruthin. (G.R. SJ 124583)

Route

1. Face Maen Huail and go right, soon passing Heol Clwyd on your left. Go ahead along Prior Street, passing St Peter's Church on your right. Bear left with Prior Street to reach Park Road. Cross this carefully and take a gate ahead to follow the signposted public footpath. Bear left and cross a footbridge over the River Clwyd.

2. Turn right to follow the signposted path through a meadow, passing a football pitch on your left and gradually bearing away from the river on your right. Continue over a stile in the far left corner of this long meadow and walk along the left-hand edge of the next field to a gate on your left-hand side in its far corner. Turn left through this and immediately turn right to enter another field. Go ahead through gap and continue with a hedge on your right to reach a stile in the next corner. Cross this and the next field to go over a stile to the left of a gate ahead and walk with a fence on your left along the course of the now dismantled railway which linked Denbigh and Ruthin. Aim for a bridge spanning the former railway line.

3. Cross a stile beside a gate just before the bridge and immediately turn left through a gate. Reach a public footpath signpost and turn right through a gate to cross the road and continue, as signposted, over a stile beside a gate on the far side of the road. Walk along the left-hand edge of this field, continue over a stile in its far corner and along the right-hand edge of the next field. Take a gate ahead and bear slightly left.

No. 44 River Clywedog

The route map for Walk 11 - Ruthin

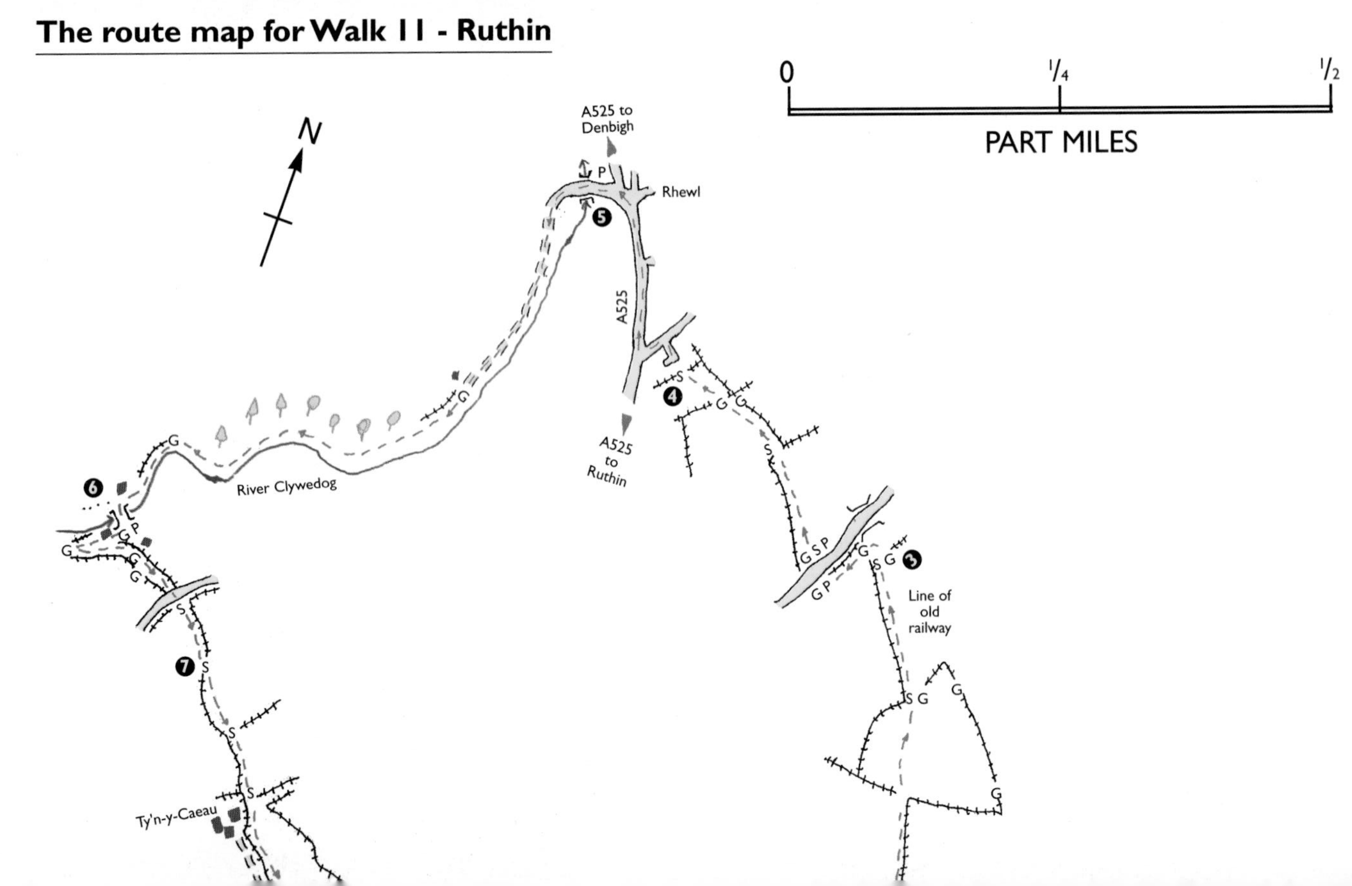

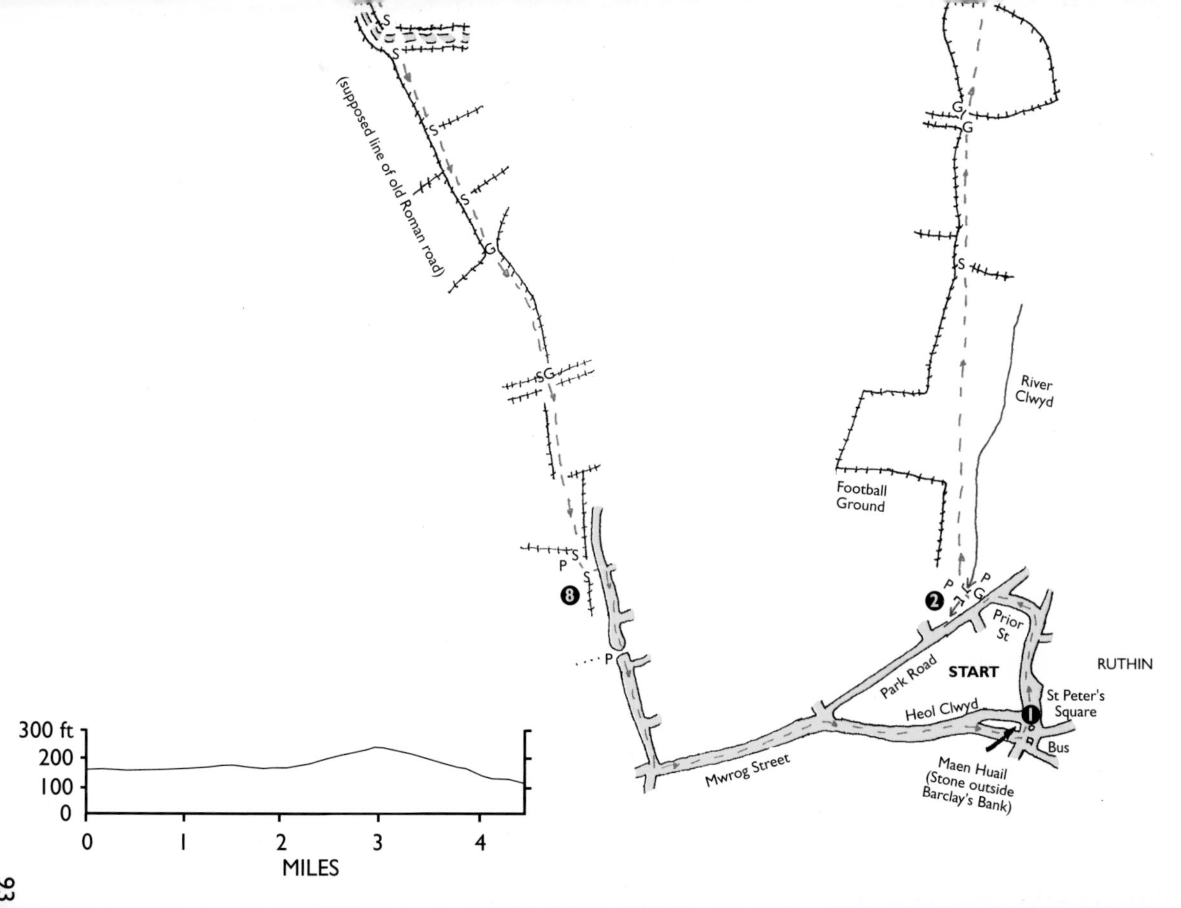
(supposed line of old Roman road)
River Clwyd
Football Ground
RUTHIN
START
Prior St
Park Road
St Peter's Square
Heol Clwyd
Bus
Mwrog Street
Maen Huail (Stone outside Barclay's Bank)
300 ft
200
100
0
0
1
2
3
4
MILES

4. Cross a stile to enter a new housing estate, Maes Derw. Go ahead to a road and turn left to join the A525. Turn right along the pavement of this main road to reach the Drovers' Arms, Rhewl, on your right. Turn left across the road and go up a No Through Road signposted as a public footpath.

5. Follow the road over a bridge across the River Clywedog and go upstream with the river on your left and the road turning into a delightful woodland track. When at a bend, notice the mysterious rock formations above the far bank of the river. Pass a house with a pretty garden on your right.

6. Turn left across a footbridge and take the gate of Melin Meredydd. Go right with the track to a hair-pin bend where you turn left to climb uphill. Go ahead through a gate and follow the lane to a road. Cross this to go ahead over a stile and follow the signposted path along the left-hand edge of a field for nearly 200 yards.

No. 45 St Mary's Church viewed from Pathway

7. Cross the stile on your left to continue in the same direction but with the hedge now on your right. The path from here to Ruthin is most probably along the line of an old Roman road. Go straight ahead along the right-hand edge of fields, over stiles and across the access lane for Ty'n-y-caeau, a farm on your right. Descend to cross an old hollow-way and continue until a metal-bar stile gives access to an estate road near a children's playground on your left.

8. Go right along the estate road to emerge at Mwrog Street. Turn left along its pavement and bear right at a fork to take Heol Clwyd, finally forking right again up Upper Clwyd Street, to return to Maen Huail.

Moel Arthur 12

There is really only the name to link this bare, rounded hill with King Arthur. It is capped by a fine example of a hillfort, complete with two deep ditches. On a clear day, there are fine views from its 1494 ft summit across the vale to Denbigh and beyond. Offa's Dyke Path makes its way along the Clwydian Range but this may have been an Arthurian frontier, too. Coarse Roman pottery has been found here, so the hill really may have played host to Arthur. Perhaps he buried a chest full of treasure on this hill. Locals speak of it and link its location with a supernatural light. When anybody who has seen the light has been brave enough to dig for the treasure, however,they have been struck senseless by a violent storm. Such storms seem to be conjured up by the guardians of sacred sites in order to discourage people digging up what shouldn't be disturbed. Sometimes the spirit of this place is more encouraging. Coming in the form a grey lady, it once awarded peas to a man and ordered him home, where they turned into gold coins.

Moel Arthur

No. 46 Summit of Moel Arthur. 1,494 ft.

Distance:	4 miles
Grid Reference:	SJ 139668
Maps:	O.S. Pathfinder 772 (Denbigh), O.S. Landranger 116 (Denbigh & Colwyn Bay).
Parking:	Car park just off and above a lane five miles east of Denbigh.
Public Transport:	The nearest bus stop is at Llangwyfan (SJ 123658), over one mile to the west of the start of this walk. Bus no 76 stops here on its way between Denbigh and Ruthin. Other buses stop in Denbigh. Telephone: 01352 704035 for details.
Refreshments:	Denbigh (five miles to the west of this walk), or bring your own!

Start: A car park on the Offa's Dyke Path north of Moel Arthur (G.R. SJ 139668)

Route

1. Descend from the car park to the lane and go right for about 150 yards. Turn left across a stile to take the signposted Offa's Dyke Path. Climb up a slope with this, bearing slightly away from the fence on your right to continue over a stile in a fence ahead.

2. Go ahead over the stile in the next fence and take the well-trodden path through the heather which meets a fence on your left. Reach a gate in this fence and turn right to divert to the hillfort and summit of Moel Arthur.

3. Retrace your steps down to the gate in the fence and turn right to resume your former direction. Bear slightly right, away from the fence, and descend to a road.

4. Go right and cross a cattle grid in the road. Leaving the Offa's Dyke Path to head south, on your left, follow the road around a bend on your right. Turn right through a gate to take the signposted public bridleway which runs around the foot of Moel Arthur, on your right, keeping beside a fence on your left. Go ahead through a gate and follow the track as it bends left.

5. Go ahead through another gate and fork left to follow the track with the fence on your left. After going ahead through three gates, this swings round to the right, going through another gate to take an enclosed track to a road.

6. Go left along the road and very soon turn right through a gate to follow a track through a forest. Bear right along a lower path at a fork and climb to cut across the track and reach the car park at the start of this walk.

No. 47 Defensive ditches protected the hillfort

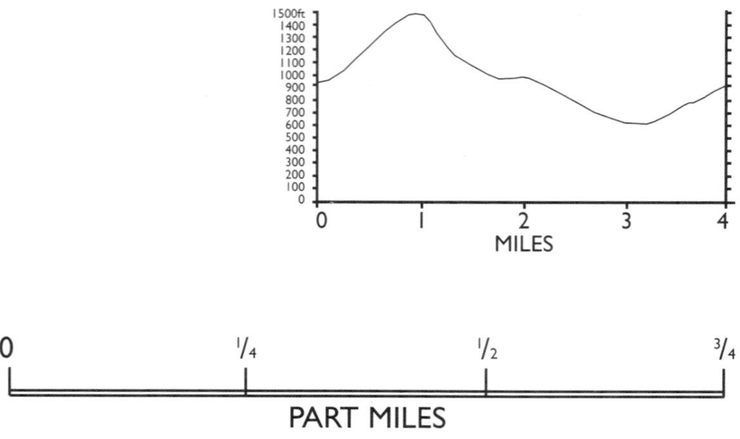

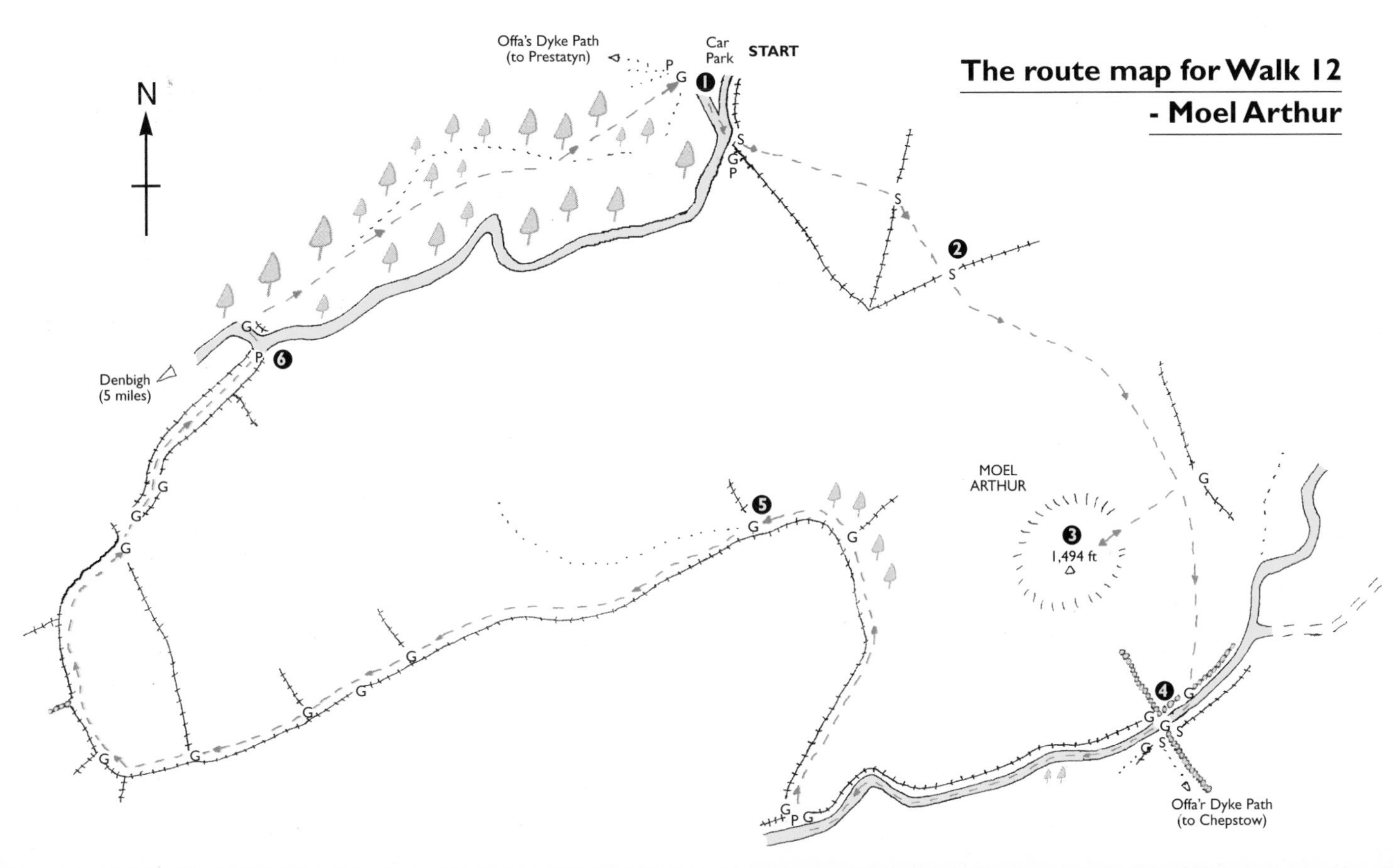

The route map for Walk 12
- Moel Arthur
N
Offa's Dyke Path
(to Prestatyn)
Car
Park
START
Denbigh
(5 miles)
MOEL
ARTHUR
1,494 ft
Offa'r Dyke Path
(to Chepstow)

No. 48 Looking south toward Offa's Dyke

Llanbadarn Fawr 13

Aberystwyth was the territory of Maelgwn Gwynedd (whom some consider to be Sir Lancelot) rather than King Arthur's. This may explain his reception here, recorded in the Life of St. Padarn. From it we know that Arthur came here and took a fancy to St. Padarn's fine tunic. Naturally, being a king, he demanded it. St. Padarn wasn't one to give away his cloak (which counted as one of the thirteen treasures of Britain), however. A cousin of St. Cadfan and St Tydecho, Padarn came to Wales with them in 516. He founded an important monastery at Llanbadarn Fawr (Celtic monastic communities were not celibate. Padarn himself had a daughter who seems to have became a female priest at Llanerfyl in Powys). The church counted as a cathedral and Padarn was its bishop. When St. David went on his famous journey to Jerusalem, St. Padarn accompanied him and was consecrated as a bishop by the Patriarch of Jerusalem. Perhaps this gave him the authority to deal with the tyrannical Arthur, who tried

to take Padarn's cloak by force. The saint ordered the earth to swallow Arthur, which it did, right up to his neck. Arthur had to beg forgiveness before Padarn released him.

Padarn was said to be handsome and a fine singer. Some think he could have been the Sandde Angel Face mentioned in the story of Culhwch and Olwen in The Mabinogion. He was so fair that none would attack him at the Battle of Camlan. Perhaps the saint had moved on from his bishopric by then

because Camlan was around the time of the great misfortunes, including the drowning of the most fertile part of Llanbadarn's diocese. This flooding was seen as a punishment, whilst is it thought that Padarn's successor was guilty of (sexual ?) misconduct. Certainly the bishopric was taken away, being absorbed into the diocese of St. Davids's.

Llanbadarn Fawr

No. 49 An effigy from a collection of stone carvings at St. Padarn's Church

Distance:	4½ miles
Grid Reference:	SN 585816
Maps:	O.S. Pathfinder 926 (Aberystwyth), O.S. Landranger 135 (Aberystwyth).
Parking:	There are car parks in Aberystwyth.
Public Transport:	Aberystwyth is the terminus for the railway from Shrewsbury and Devil's Bridge. Buses stop near the station.
Refreshments:	Aberystwyth.

No. 50 Looking south from Pen Dinas

No. 51 The beautiful stained glass window in St Padarn's Church

Start: Aberystwyth railway station is in the centre of town, near the bus stops and car parks. (G.R. SN 585816)

Route

1. With your back to the railway station, go right. Turn right through the gates of Plas-crug and take the signposted way towards Aberystwyth's swimming pool as far as a junior school on your right.

2. Turn right to pass the school on your right and approach the railway line. Do not cross it. Turn left to walk parallel to the railway and past rugby pitches on your left. Turn left in the far corner, join a lane and emerge with it on Padarn Crescent. Go right along its pavement and reach St. Padarn' s Church on your left.

3. Continue past St. Padarn's Church, on your left. Turn right at a crossroads and cross both the main line and the narrow gauge railways. Turn left through a gate along the signposted footpath to the Afon Rheidol.

4. Turn right to walk downstream with the river on your left. When you reach a road bridge, cross the river by it and continue past the first road on your right. Soon after it, take a short path on your right to join a higher road. Follow this until house no 58, on your left.

5. Turn left up steps between house nos. 56 and 58. Follow Bryn Place to reach the main A487 and turn left along its pavement as far as the post office and a pedestrian crossing.

6. Turn right across the road and take the lane ahead, soon passing The Tollgate pub on your left. Turn right up a track just before Gorwel Deg. Climb with the enclosed track to a stile, cross it and take the middle path ahead, contouring around the hillside of Pen Dinas. Descend to a lane at a signpost.

7. Go right along the lane until a signpost on your left shows where you bear left over a stile and take an enclosed path towards the harbour. Go right with the harbour lane back to the main A487 road. Turn left along its pavement past the fire station on your left and across the bridge over the Afon Rheidol. Bear right to take Mill Street back towards the railway station.

Cerrig Meibion Arthur

14

The Mabinogion, that great body of ancient Welsh literature, tells in the story of Culhwch and Olwen how King Arthur came to the Preseli Hills to fight the Twrch Trwyth. These enemies of Arthur probably had a boar as their symbol and some say they were Irish, others that they were Vandals. What is clear is that the Twrch Trwyth fought King Arthur at Cwm Cerwyn. Gwydre, son of Arthur, was slain and so, presumably, was a second son, with important bearings on the succession and the tragedy of Camlan. As proof, there are two standing stones known as the Stones of the Sons of Arthur.

Also on this walk is the stone enclosure known as Bedd Arthur. This appears to be rectangular in shape

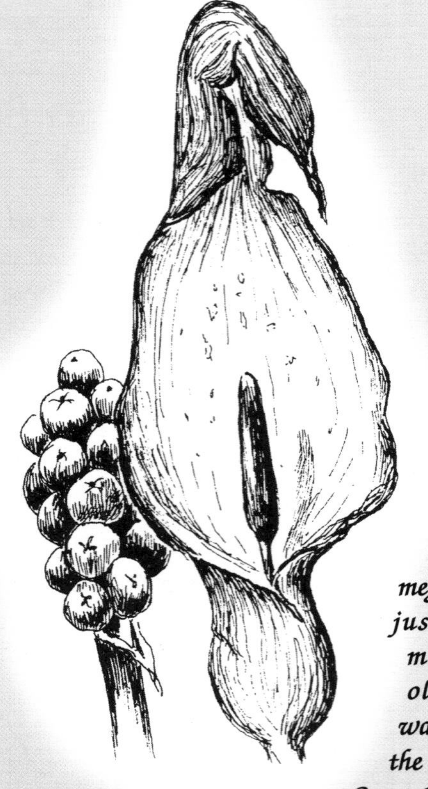

but it is actually an ellipse with all the characteristics recognised by Professor Alexander Thom. The major axis is 27 megalithic yards, the minor axis 10 megalithic yards and the interfocal distances 25 megalithic yards. The perimeter is just over the required 60 megalithic yards. It is much older than a sixth-century warrior chieftain, of course, but the mystical Arthur who was the Great Bear (Arth Fawr) would have appeared in the sky as the pole star to whoever built this monument.

The Preselis would be the place for the mystical Arthur to put in an appearance, for these are magical hills. The entrance to the Celtic Underworld known as Annwn is here, on the sacred peak of Carn Ingli and in Glyn Cych. Arthur harrowed hell, freeing the prisoners of Annwn, being the Aradr of Taliesin's poem Spoils of Annwn. To the Celts, heaven and hell were the same place, with the difference being in your ability to handle the situation.

Cerrig Meibion Arthur

No. 52 The stone enclosure known as Beddarthur

Distance: 11½ miles

Grid Reference: SN 076295

Maps: O.S. Pathfinders 1033 (Newport & Eglwyswrw) and 1057 (Ambleston & Llandissilio), O.S. Landranger 145 (Cardigan)

Parking: There is a car park below the Old Post Office, Rosebush.

Public Transport: Trains no longer run to this exalted spot. It may be possible to come on an infrequent bus from Fishguard (tel. 01267 231817). If so, you would need to stay the night to complete this walk. There's no better place to stay than the Old Post Office (tel. 01437 532205).

Refreshments: Rosebush.

No. 53 The standing stones of the sons of King Arthur

Start: The Old Post Office, Rosebush. (G.R. SN 076295)

Route

1. With your back to the Old Post Office and with the telephone box at your side, go right along the lane. Pass the entrance to the Tafarn Sinc Preseli on your right and soon turn left up the access lane for Pant-mawr. This is waymarked with a yellow arrow. Climb with the track through the farmyard, bear left and immediately right. Climb with an enclosed track to a gate. Go through this and bear left, keeping a fence on your left. Go ahead through a gap and turn right with a fence and a line of trees on your right. Continue over a stile in the corner and along the right-hand edge of the next field to a stile giving access to an old green track.

2. Turn left along this track. Walk past a conifer forest on your left, then with an open space between you and the trees on your left, then beside the forest again. Pass another open space where the forest is recessed on your left, then walk beside the forest again and through a gate ahead. Bear right away from the forest to follow the path to the 1760ft summit of Foel Cwmcerwyn.

3. Bear slightly left as you go ahead from the summit of Foel Cwmcerwyn, so that you meet the forest on your left where there is a stile in a corner formed by a fence ahead. Cross this stile and bear right to join the old Golden Road, the prehistoric path along the ridge of the Preselis.

4. Go right along the Golden Road for two miles. Pass a valley running south on your right and note where the track turns off to run down it. Continue for nearly one more mile to pass the rocks of Carn Bica on your left and, in about 100 yards, come to Bedd Arthur.

5. Retrace your steps from Bedd Arthur to the valley running south, which is now on your left. Turn left down the track running along the left-hand side of this valley. Continue to descend to where a distinct path comes in sharply from your right.

6. Turn sharply right along this grassy track and come to a roughly surfaced lane. The standing stones known as Cerrig Meibion Arthur are across some more moorland on the far side of this lane. Turn left along this lane as you face the standing stones, or right if you have visited the standing stones and retraced your steps to the lane. Follow the lane to a road.

7. Turn right along the road. Follow it around a bend on your left and pass two turnings on your left before you eventually come to a T junction ahead. Turn right along the B4313, as signposted for Fishguard. Pass a rough track on your right which becomes the track

No. 54 The Old Post Office, Rosebush

that led you towards Foel Cwmcerwyn at the start of this walk. Take the next turning on your right to follow the road back to Rosebush and the Old Post Office, with its licensed restaurant, bistro and tea-rooms.

The route map for Walk 14 - Cerrig Meibion Arthur

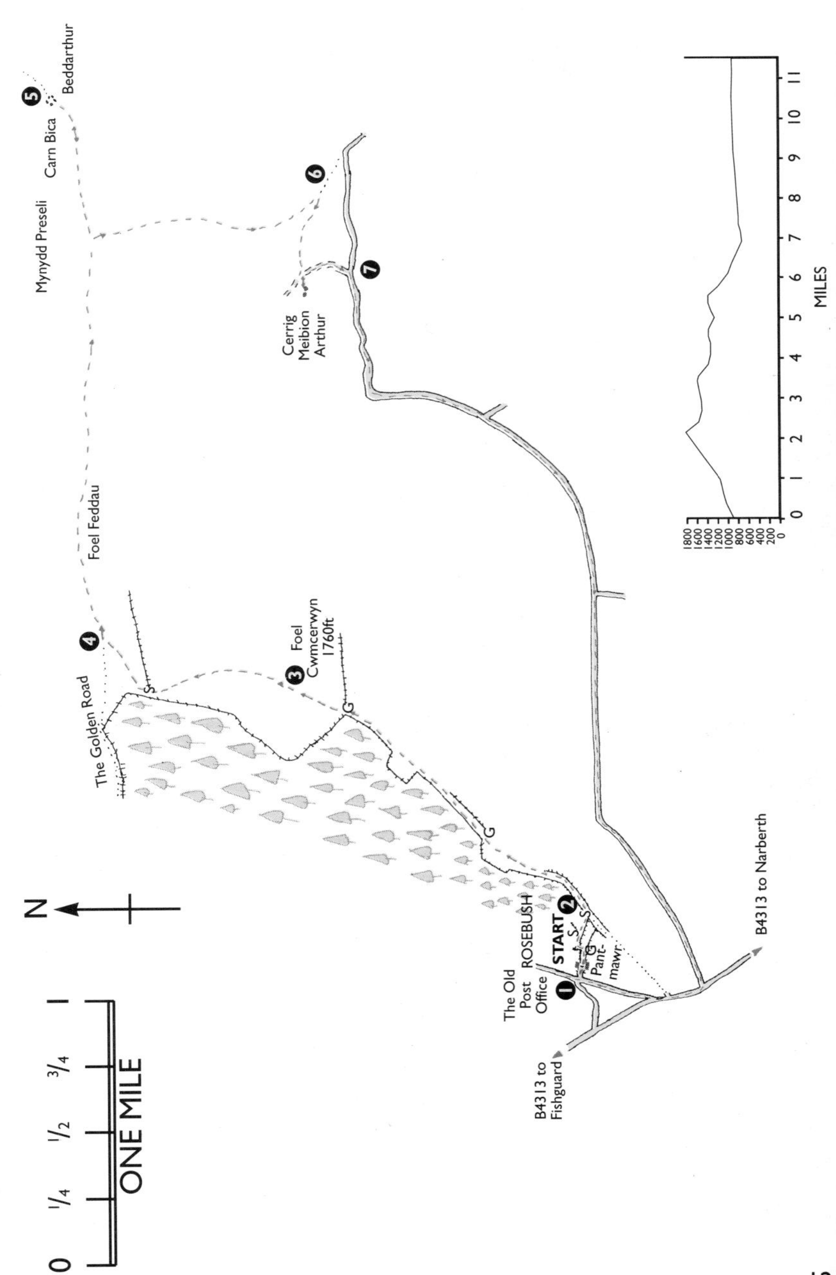

No. 55 Carn Bica

Knucklas 15

King Arthur had three queens, all named Gwynhwyfar (Guinevere). There is a local tradition that the second of these Gwynhwyfars married Arthur from the castle at Knucklas. Her father was Ogfran Gawr, who asked for Arthur's aid in releasing his two sons from captivity at the hands of giants from Shropshire. He rewarded Arthur for his help by giving him his daughter as a new queen. The first Gwynhwyfar was getting too old to bear Arthur the new heirs he needed after the loss of his sons at Cwm Cerwyn (see Walk 14). Ogfran Gawr was of giant blood and when a mound near Monaughty Poeth (SO 255747) was excavated in the 19th century, five skeletons of exceptional size were found in it. Arthur's second Gwynhwyfar brought him shame, however, by carrying on an affair with Medrawt, most probably the Medrawt who was the son of St Cawrdaf son of Caradoc Vreichfras, rather than the Medrawt who was the son of Llew son of Cynfarch Oer, who was probably the enemy of Arthur at Camlan. The grave of Gwynhwyfar, the daughter of Ogfran Gawr, has been located in Perthshire, where King Arthur's war dogs caught up with the fleeing lovers and tore Gwynhwyfar to pieces.

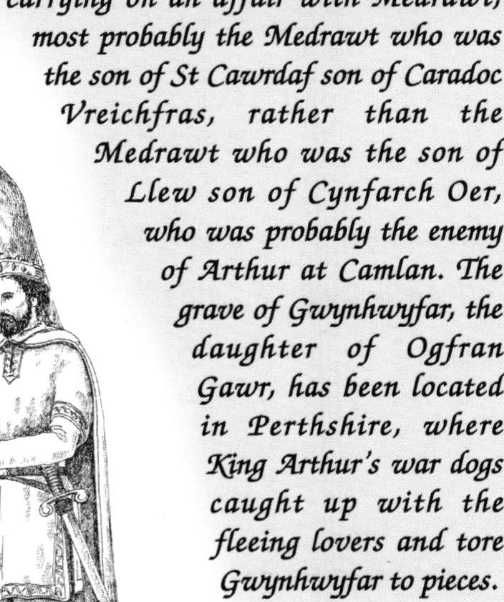

Knucklas

No. 56 Facing west from the remains of Cnwclas Castle

Distance:	4 miles
Grid Reference:	SO 255741
Maps:	O.S. Pathfinder 950 (Knighton & Brampton Bryan), O.S. Landranger 137 (Ludlow & Wenlock Edge) or 148 (Presteigne & Hay-on-Wye).
Parking:	Parking is possible in the streets near Knucklas railway station.
Public Transport:	Ride the scenic Heart of Wales Line (Swansea - Shrewsbury) and alight at Knucklas railway station.
Refreshments:	There is a pub and a shop at Knucklas.

Start: Knucklas railway station (G.R. SO 255741)

Route

1. With your back to the railway line, go ahead down the road known as Glyndwr, passing a housing estate on your left. Go left at a T-junction and fork right to pass the Castle Inn on your left. Turn right over a bridge across the Ffrwdwen Brook. Pass the village stores and post office on your left and fork left to walk along a lane above the railway on your left and below Cnwclas Castle on your right.

2. When the lane bends to the right, turn sharply right to take a footpath above the steep bank on your right, keeping a fence on your left. Just after another fence and hedge comes in at a right angle on your left, cross over the non-barbed wire fence as you turn left, then soon turn right to follow a path which spirals up to the top of the old castle hill.

3. Retrace your steps to the bend in the lane. With the railway on your left, ignore the lane bending right and go straight ahead. Turn left over a stile, continue with care across the railway track and take another stile on its far side. Turn right to walk along the top of the field. Go ahead over a stile in the next corner and bear left down to a footbridge over the Ffrwdwen Brook.

4. Go ahead through the meadow to a road and turn right along it to reach a T-junction at Heyop. Turn left along a lane which passes Cleobury Farm on your left. Follow this lane for nearly one mile, passing a gate giving access to Llangwyn on your right. After passing a wooded slope on your left, climb to where two field gates face each other on opposite sides of the lane.

5. Turn sharply left through the gate and follow a track running beside a fence on your left. Go ahead through a gate in the top corner and continue over the ridge to descend to a small gate in the bottom

No. 57 Cwm Jenkin

left-hand corner of this field, above the farm buildings of Cwm Jenkin.

6. Descend with the farm access lane to walk with a brook on your right. This brook switches to your left just before Lower Dolwilkin but soon returns to your right as you go down the valley to join a road.

7. Turn right into Knucklas, following the road under the railway viaduct and forking left towards the bridge across the brook. Don't cross this, but pass it on your left as you retrace your steps to the railway station.

The route map for Walk 15 - Knucklas

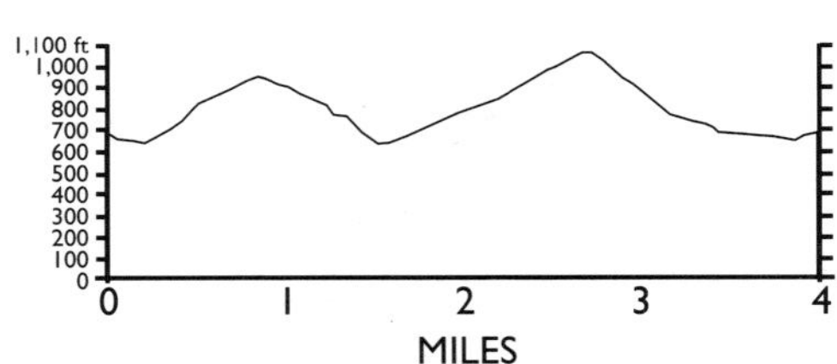

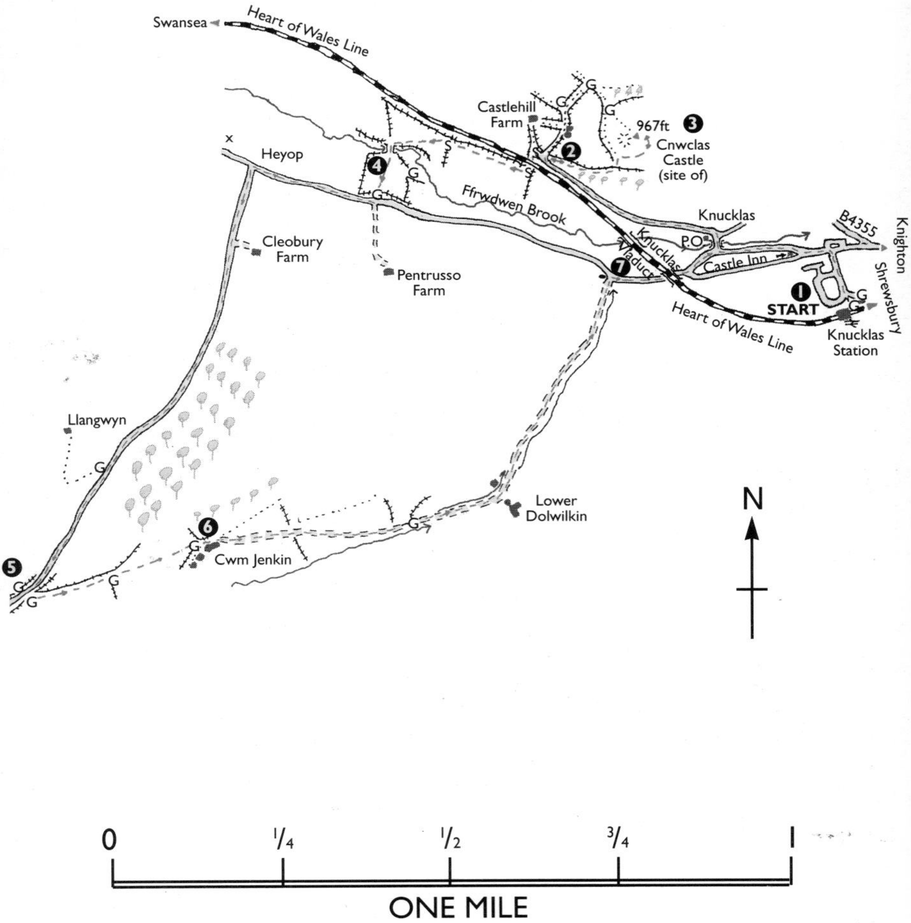

Swansea
Heart of Wales Line
Castlehill Farm
967ft
Cnwclas Castle (site of)
Heyop
Ffrwdwen Brook
Knucklas
P.O.
Castle Inn
B4355
Knighton
Shrewsbury
Cleobury Farm
Pentrusso Farm
Knucklas Viaduct
START
Heart of Wales Line
Knucklas Station
Llangwyn
Lower Dolwilkin
N
Cwm Jenkin

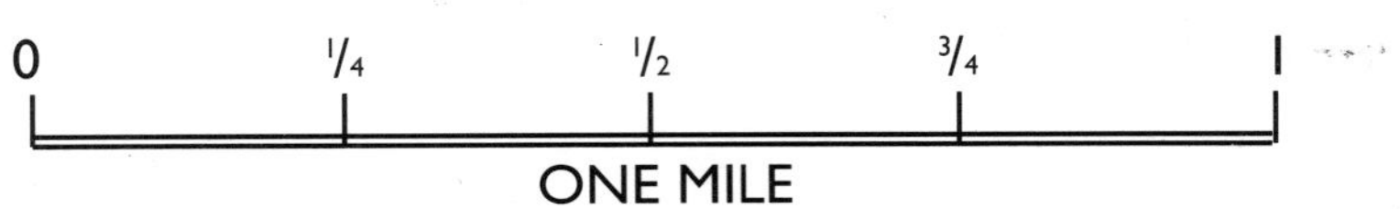

No. 58 Viaduct

No. 59 Viaduct as seen from the site of the Cnwclas Castle

Cilgerran 16

Tracing the story of King Arthur is a bit like assembling a jigsaw with just a few of its pieces. Various researchers make the pieces fit their particular theories. The location of Arthurian battles is a favourite arena for discussion. The Battle of Llongborth, which preceded Camlan, has been located at Portsmouth, Langport and at Porth-is-Coed in Gwent. There is another candidate, in Dyfed, which is featured in Walk 17.

One key to where Llongborth really was is in the Welsh elegy praising Geraint. Written by Llywarch Hen (who lived throughout the Arthurian period and attained well over 100 years), it tells how:

> In Llongborth Geraint was slain.
> Heroes of the land of Dyfneint,
> Before they were slain, they slew.

There was more than one Geraint in power in those days, but it was probably Geraint ap Erbin, the ruler of Domnonia (Devon and Cornwall). It seems that this Geraint could also have held land in Dyfed, for Jonathan Caredig Davies recorded in his book Folklore of West and Mid-Wales (1911) that the spot where the remains of the castle now stand was known in ancient times as Dyngeraint, so named from Geraint, one of King Arthur's knights.' Cilgerran is only seven miles from Penbryn, which the same researcher noted as the location of the Battle of Llongborth.

Cilgerran Castle is, of course, medieval. The beautiful Nest probably left her husband Gerald of Windsor here in order

to run off with Owain ap Cadwgan – but that's another story! Now in the care of Cadw, Cilgerran Castle is well worth a visit and has its own guidebook.

Cilgerran

No. 60 Cilgerran Castle

Distance:	$6\frac{1}{2}$ miles
Grid Reference:	SN 197429
Maps:	O.S. Pathfinders 1010 (Cardigan & Dinas Head) and 1011 (Newcastle Emlyn), O.S. Landranger 145 (Cardigan).
Parking:	There is a car park at the start of this walk, near the Coracle Centre at Cilgerran.
Public Transport:	Bus no 430 runs to Cilgerran from Cardigan and Crymych. Telephone 01267 231817 for details.
Refreshments:	Cilgerran

No. 61 Pathway to Cilgerran Castle

Start: The Coracle Centre car park near the riverside below Cilgerran. (G.R. SN 197429)

Route

1. Face the river and go left alongside the river on your right. Fork left up a signposted path for the castle and village. Turn left when you reach the castle and go right to emerge on a lane near the castle's entrance on your right. Bear left to the main road running through Cilgerran, reaching the Castle Kitchen restaurant, where buses stop.

2. Go right and soon pass the school on your right. Turn left with a signposted track which cuts across the line of a dismantled railway and heads for the farm of Penrallt Fach.

3. As you approach the farm, bear right over a stile to take the waymarked path below it. Go ahead through a gap in the hedge and take a gate when level with the farm, on your left. Turn right down an enclosed path to a stream, which you ford.

4. Bear left along the left-hand edges of three fields then cross a field diagonally to its far right corner. Go ahead over a stile and turn right to emerge over another stile onto a muddy track. Go left along this, follow it round a bend on your right and, soon, cross a stile on your left.

5. Climb uphill to a stile in the top right-hand corner of the field. Cross it and turn left up a firm track which bends right and reaches a crosstracks. Turn left along a farm access track.

6. Fork right over a stile to pass the farm buildings on your left. Continue along the left-hand edge of the next field and bear left over a stile as you approach a gate in the corner ahead. Bear right to cross another stile and keep the buildings of Ty-hên on your right. Go over a stile beside a gate in the fence ahead and bear right to reach a walled track. Turn left down towards a stream, take a stile on your left to reach a footbridge and turn right across this.

7. Climb up the left-hand edge of the pasture, cross a stile on your left, turn right and reach an access lane. Go left along this to a road. Turn left and almost immediately turn right at a road junction.

8. Turn right along a firm track which is signposted as a public footpath. Follow this path through woodland, keeping near the fence, wall or hedge on your left. Go down a waymarked hairpin bend on your right, then turn left to walk through forest above a stream on your right.

9. Turn left just before a gate, climb to a stile and turn right to cross it and pass above a house on your right. Join a track which passes the next house on

No. 62
Afon Teifi

your left, then bear left to climb above the next building and follow the path along the foot of a forest. This eventually leads to a road.

10. Go left along the road, then turn right at the road junction on the edge of Cilgerran.

11. Turn left down the signposted public footpath beside the Masons Arms. Follow this path as it bends right, then turn left to descend to the level of the River Teifi and walk with the river on your right back to the Coracle Centre.

No. 63 Afon Teifi as seen from the Coracle Centre

The route map for Walk 16 - Cilgerran

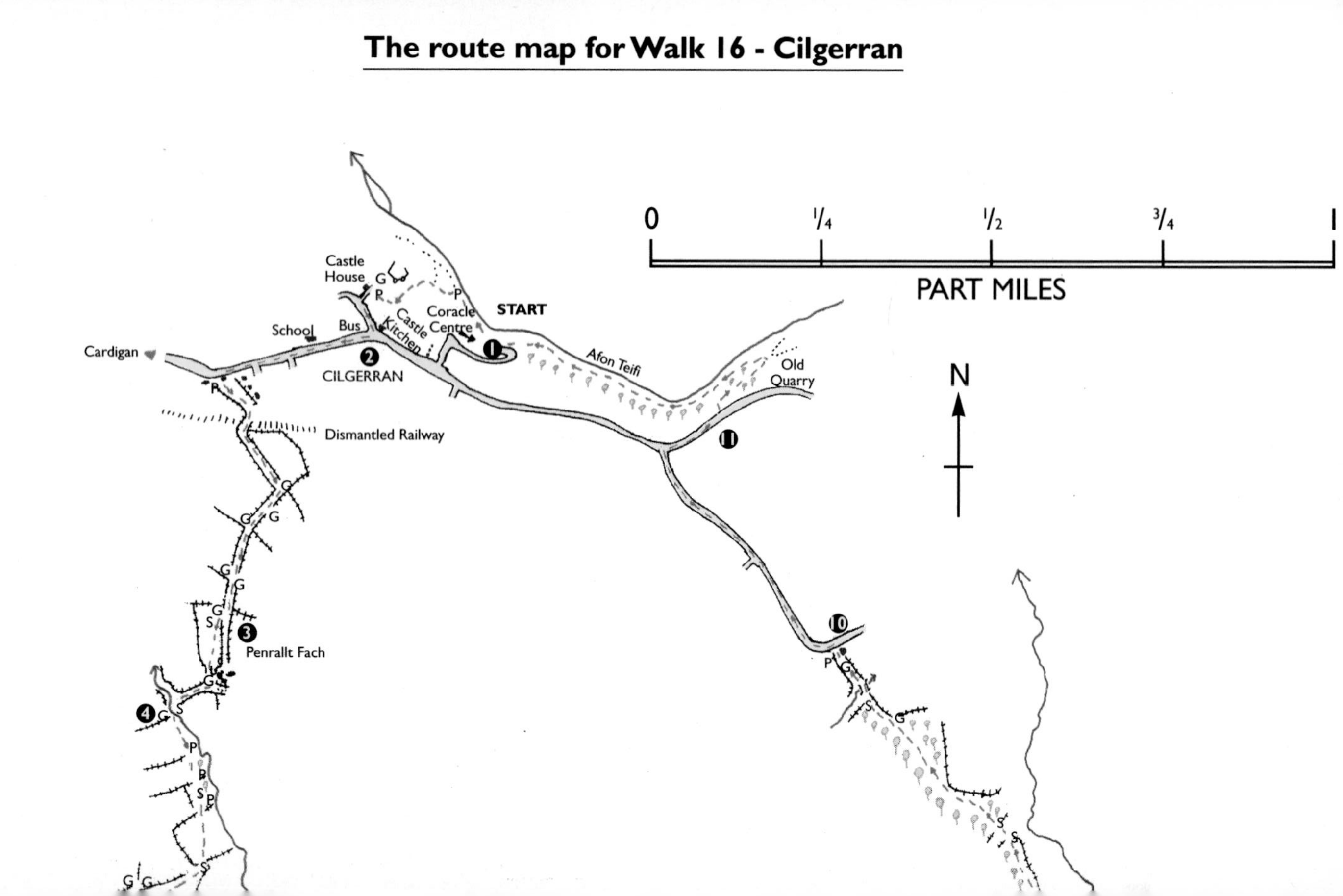

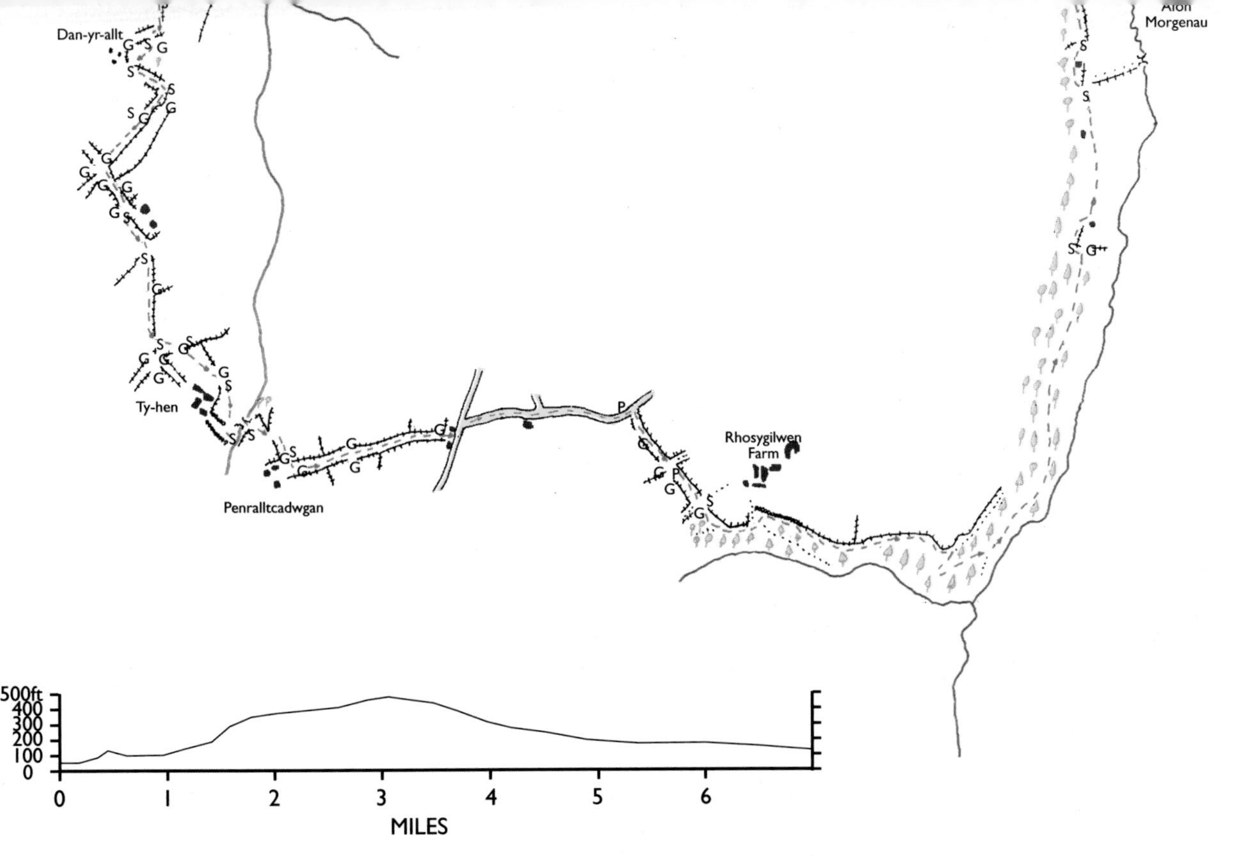

Morgenau
Dan-yr-allt
Ty-hen
Penralltcadwgan
Rhosygilwen Farm
500ft
400
300
200
100
0
0
1
2
3
4
5
6
MILES

No. 64 View of Afon Teifi as seen from the keep of Cilgerran Castle

Penbryn 17

There is a tradition, recorded by Jonathan Ceredig Davies in his Folklore of West and Mid-Wales (1911), that the Battle of Llongborth was fought at Penbryn. There is a farm in this parish called Perth Geraint, where Geraint, one of Arthur's knights who was killed in the battle, was buried. This is the "comely and graceful" Geraint, as described by Tennyson, who married the young Lady Enid.

Sir Geraint may have been leading King Arthur's forces on an assault of a beach near Penbryn. Arthur may have sailed here from Brittany on his way to deal with his treacherous upstart of a

nephew Medrawt. The campaign may have led northward along the old Roman road of Sarn Helen towards its tragic climax at Camlan.

Penbryn is certainly a special spot. Unseen hands took the stones overnight to ensure the supernatural location of the old church, dedicated to St. Michael. A standing stone at grid reference SN 289513 is inscribed "Corbalengi iacit Ordovs", commemorating Carbalengus of the Ordovices tribe of Mid Wales.

This is much earlier than King Arthur's reign if we go by the date of the first century AD gold coin that was found under this stone, along with a burial urn, with weapons and bones being discovered close by.

There is a stone near Troed-y-Rhiw which, according to tradition, was an ejected pebble from the clog of a giant who lived in the district in ancient times.

The strategic nature of this area is still recognised by the nearby missile-testing base at Aberporth.

Penbryn

No. 65 Carreg-y-Ty, overlooking Traeth Bach

Grid Reference: SN 296522 **Distance:** 4¾ miles

Maps: O.S. Pathfinder 988 (New Quay & Aberporth), O.S. Landranger 145 (Cardigan).

Parking: There is a car park at the start of this walk and another at St. Michael's Church, Penbryn.

Public Transport: Both the no. 550 and no. 551 buses from Cardigan will take you near the start of this walk. Bring an O.S. map to follow the route between the bus stop and Penbryn. Tel 01267 231817.

Refreshments: There is a seasonal cafe (Cartws Cafe) at the start of this walk, while pubs and shops are open all year in Llangranog.

No. 66 Ynys Lochtyn from Carreg-y-Tŷ

Start: The Car Park, Penbryn. (G.R. SN 296522)

Route

1. Go left from the car park, passing Cartws Cafe on your left. Go ahead through a gate and turn right along the signposted public footpath up a track towards a hillside (signposted for Capel Penmorfa and Llangranog).

2. Bear left at the fork to climb gradually with the track which affords views over the beach and bay on your left. When you reach a gate across the track, bear left over a stile to follow the waymarked clifftop path, keeping the sea on your left. Continue past a radio mast on your right and descend, as waymarked.

3. Turn right to go down steps, as waymarked. Cross a stile in the bottom of the valley and cross the stream

to climb up steps on the other side. Go over a stile to enter a field and follow the waymarked path around its left-hand edge. Climb to pass the earthwork of Castell-bach on your right.

4. Go ahead over a stile to walk along the coastal path, with the sea on your left, towards Llangranog.

5. Meet a road at a hairpin bend and bear right uphill, away from Llangranog. Pass the entrance to Maes-y-Morfa on your left, then the farm buildings of Morfa-Uchaf. Ignore a road turning on your left, then the access lane to Morfa Canol on your right. Don't be misled into taking the next hedged track on your right, when the road bends left.

6. Turn right along an old green lane which is hedged on both sides at first. Continue through a gate ahead and pass through woodland to reach the signposted path junction where you turn left to retrace your steps to the start of this walk. Extend it by going ahead to the road and turning right to climb up to St. Michael's Church.

7. Retrace your steps downhill back to the car park at the start of this walk.

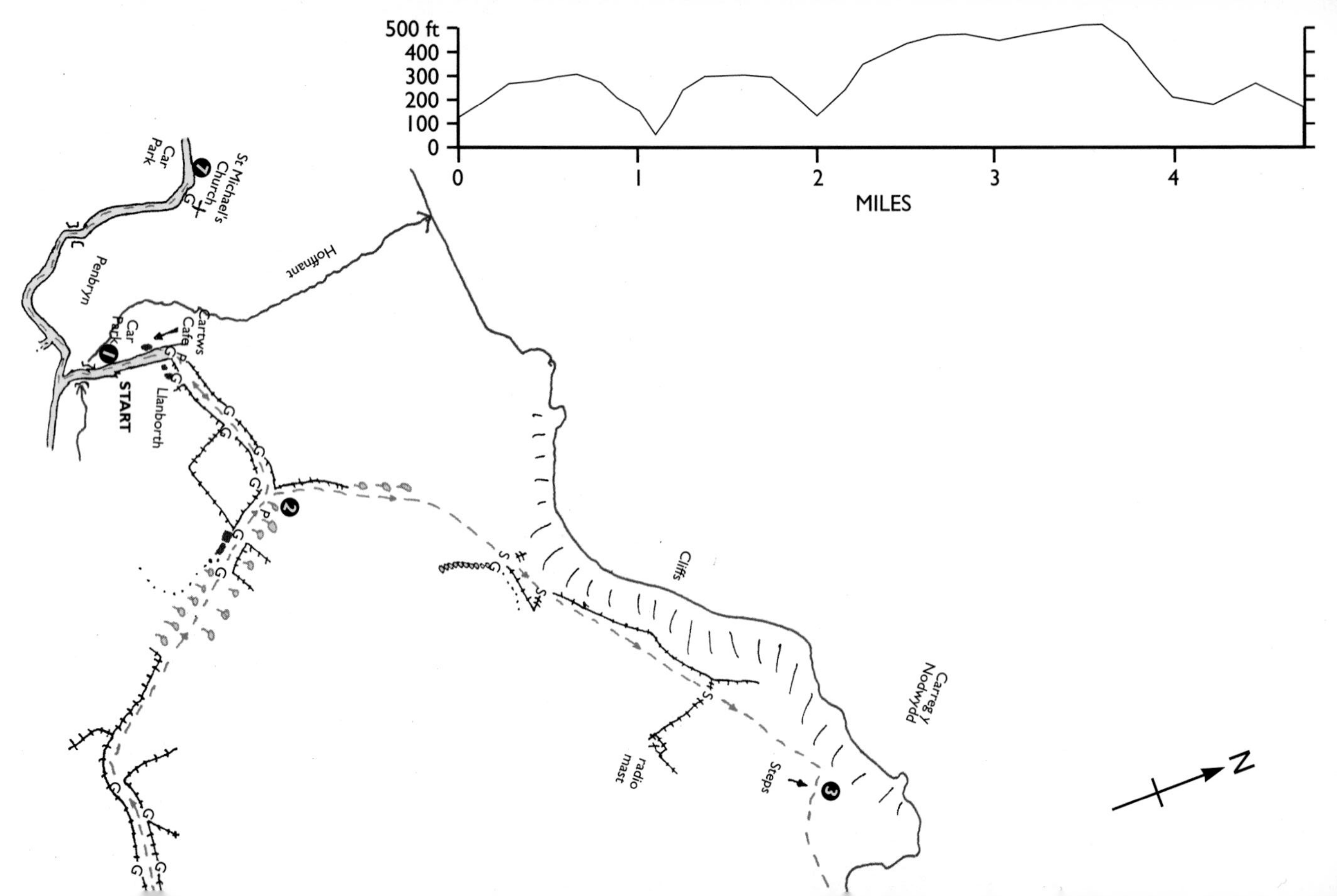

500 ft
400
300
200
100
0
0
1
2
3
4
MILES
N
Carreg y Nodwydd
Steps
Cliffs
radio mast
Hoffnant
St Michael's Church
Car Park
Cartws Cafe
Llanborth
Car Park
START
Penbryn

The route map for Walk 17 - Penbryn

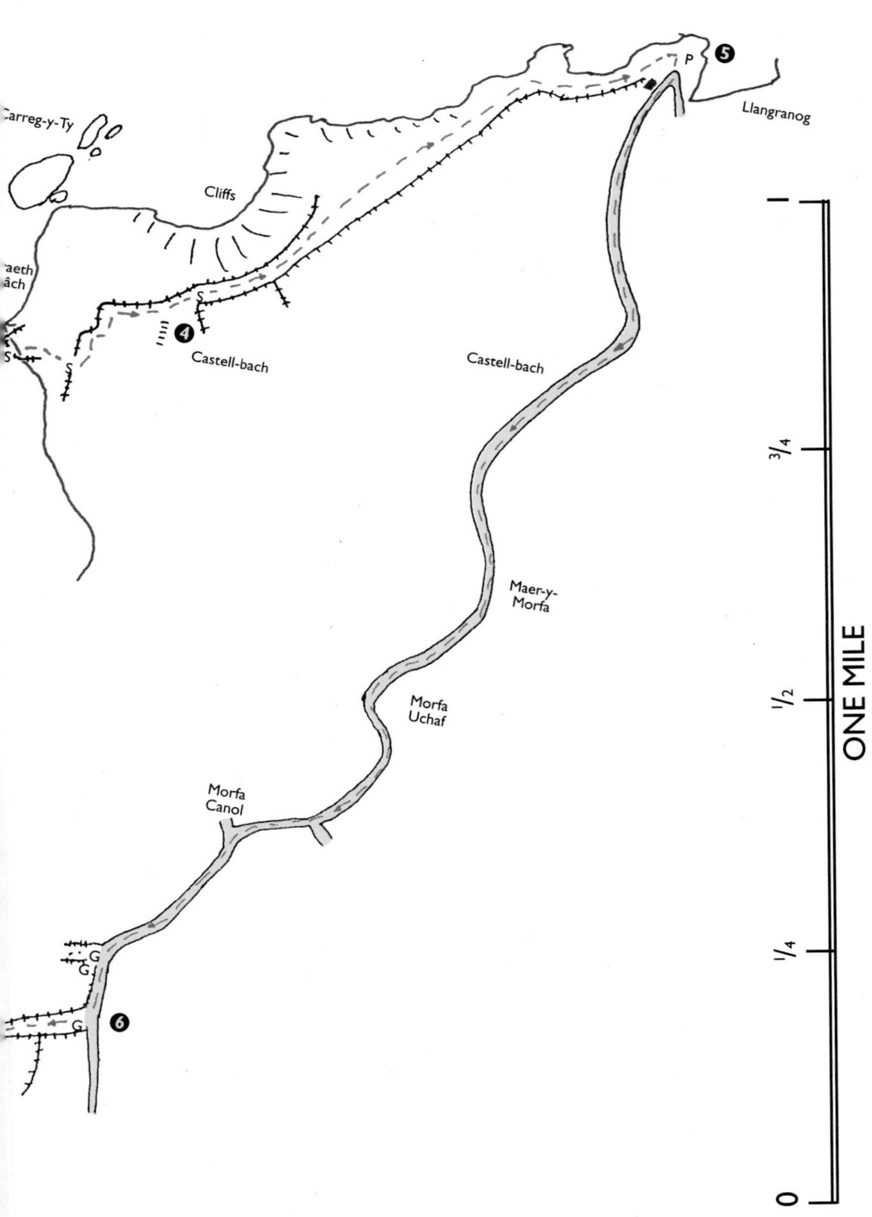

No. 67 From cliff-top path, looking south-wet across beach

Camlan 18

The story of Arthur draws to a close at Camlan. The Annales Cambriae date this battle to 537, but that may mean 537 years from Jesus' crucifixion. It was around the time of plague, famine and earthquakes, perhaps caused by some celestial body's close proximity to the earth. The triumphant Britons had quarrelled amongst themselves, with Sir Lancelot (Maelgwn Gwynedd?) involved with Queen Gwynhwyfar. King Arthur may have fathered a new son and heir (Morgan – born across the sea in Brittany?) by a new, younger, Gwynhwyfar. This may have disappointed his nephew and foster-son Medrawt, who may even have been his own son by an incestuous union with his sister Gwyar (Morgan-le-Faye?). Seeing his ambition to succeed Arthur slip from his grasp, Medrawt was probably talked into leading a rebellion and even recruited Saxon allies.

The two armies converged at Camlan, traditionally

located between Dinas Mawddwy and Mallwyd, near the border of Gwynedd with Powys. This was a strategic spot, where the old Roman road from Wroxeter to Brithdir (linking with Sarn Helen) crossed the River Dyfi, probably near where the 17th century packhorse bridge can be seen at the Meirion Mill. Place names tell the story and Medrawt's Saxon allies slept the night before the battle near Nant-y-saeson (SH 921130). The battle probably took place in November, the month of death. One of the Three Frivolous Battles of Britain, it was started by accident. A nervous soldier drew his sword to kill an adder, thus provoking the fighting when a parley was being arranged. It was important to cleanse this place of civil war, so a memorial stone was erected just within the grounds of the Meirion Mill and at the edge of the battlefield in 1994. The reincarnation of King Arthur unveiled it on 4th July, with a druid to bless it. Local children laid a posy of flowers and read poetry.

> On Camlan's field a stone we raise,
> That it may wield our note of praise
> And lay to rest the adder's work,
> With all the woe that strife imparts.
> Time has healed the wounds of Arthur,
> Forgiven Medrawt for the slaughter.
> Together now, with one accord,
> We acknowledge Arthur as our lord.
> Truth, honour, justice, must once again
> Ride triumphant in his reign.

The battle started at Maes-y-camlan, where the stream Nant y Gamell may have been rendered into the English River Camel that

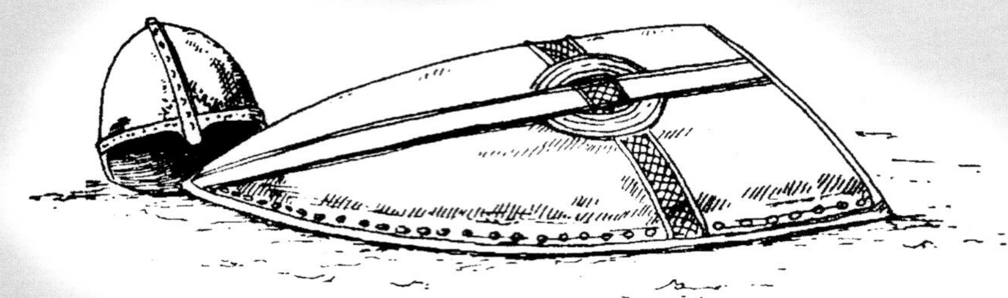

misled Tennyson to Camelford in Cornwall (where the Britons did fight the Saxons, but in the ninth century). The wounded were laid to rest on Bryn-Cleifion, near the end of this walk. The fighting moved up the valley of the River Cerist, a tributary of the Dyfi, towards the Mawddach estuary. Perhaps Arthur was taken by boat from Arthog to Bardsey after the battle. He was grievously wounded (made impotent by what was euphemistically termed a blow to the thigh). Medrawt was killed. One of the few to survive the battle with credit was Derfel Gadarn, who became the patron saint of Llandderfel, near Bala. Osfran, whose son's grave is at Camlan (perhaps shared with the Gwylliaid Cochion Mawddwy at Collfryn, SH 887118), is linked in a 12th century poem with Tywyn, also in Meirionnydd. Perhaps he was related to Morfran son of Tegid (with Llyn Tegid being Bala Lake).

The church at Mallwyd was founded in the early sixth century by St Tydecho, a nephew of King Arthur. His mother was Anna of Gwent, Arthur's sister. Tydecho's paternal grandfather was Emyr Llydaw, the ruler of Brittany who is linked with Ambrosius Aurelianus, Myrddin Emrys (Merlin) and the opposition to Vortigern (see Walk 1, Dinas Emrys).

The only people to benefit from the Battle of Camlan were the Saxons. Perhaps less talented, but more disciplined, the invaders broke through at the Battle of Dyrham, north of Bath, in 577 A.D., perhaps not long after the correct date for Camlan. The Welsh were soon divided from the Cornish and England was created. Despite the triumph of Henry Tudor in 1485, English language and culture came to dominate Britain. Welsh could still be the language of London and Oxford if the Battle of Camlan had been avoided and the Celtic golden age earned by Arthur's earlier victories over the Saxons sustained.

No. 68 King Arthur's memorial stone

Camlan

Grid Reference:	SH 859139 **Distance:** 5 ¼ miles
Maps:	O.S. Outdoor Leisure 23 (Snowdonia: Cadair Idris area), O.S. Landrangers 124 (Dolgellau) or 125 (Bala & Lake Vyrnwy).
Parking:	In the Meirion Mill when open, or the lay-bys beside the A470 north of the turning to Aberangell (between the two garages) and at Mallwyd (near point 5).
Public Transport:	Buses to Buckley Pines Hotel, near the Meirion Mill, Dinas Mawddwy, from Dolgellau (no 33) and from Machynlleth (no 518). Tel 01286 679535 for details.
Refreshments:	The Old Station Coffee Shop, Meirion Mill, Brigands Inn and the garage at Mallwyd.

No. 69 Afon Dyfi, as seen from Maes-y-Camlan

Start The Meirion Mill is on the A470 one mile north of its junction with the A458 at Mallwyd, about 11 miles east of Dolgellau (G.R. SH 859139)

Route

1. The Meirion Mill is open on a seasonal basis, usually from March to November (tel. 01650 531311). WHEN OPEN, go to the far end of the car park and take the gate giving access to the course of the dismantled railway. Follow this to the memorial stone to King Arthur on the edge of the battlefield of Camlan. Retrace your steps to the Old Station Coffee Shop and turn sharply left just before it to a stile in the corner. Cross this stile and the field to reach another stile in the left-hand corner ahead. This stile gives access to a minor road. WHEN

CLOSED, go left from the Meirion Mill's entrance, away from the river. Turn sharply left along the minor road to Aberangell.

2. Go left along the minor road, soon crossing a stream, Nant Minllyn. Look out for the memorial stone on your left. Pass Quarry Cottages on your right and turn right with the signposted public footpath which crosses the stream Nant y Gamell in the farmyard at Camlan.

3. Turn left to take a gate and walk across the sloping field of Maes-y-Camlan, keeping the fence and the view over the river on your left. Continue over a stile across open, sloping, pasture and cross another stile before fording a stream. Fork left to follow the path between trees and down to the minor road, on your left.

4. Go left down the road. Before turning right over the bridge (Pont Mallwyd), go ahead to see a waterfall in the River Dyfi on your right. Return to the bridge and use it to cross the river. Follow this lane to Mallwyd and visit St Tydecho's Church, going right from the roundabout.

5. Return to the roundabout and go right to pass the Brigands Inn on your right. Fork right just before a garage to take a farm access lane. Pass farm buildings on your right, take the gate ahead and follow the lane when it turns right.

6. Turn left, off the lane, down a track, soon going through a gate. Continue to a second gate but don't go through it. Bear left, as waymarked, just before it, down through woodland to the River Cleifion. Go left, above the river on your right, to the A458 road. Turn right across a bridge over the river.

7. Leave the A458 by turning left up a lane. Go left at the next junction and almost immediately right to follow a lane across the stream Nant Cwm Cewydd.

8. Turn sharply left to take the signposted path which is

No. 70 Maes-y-Camlan

No. 71 Foxgloves and wild strawberries

The route map for Walk 18 - Camlan

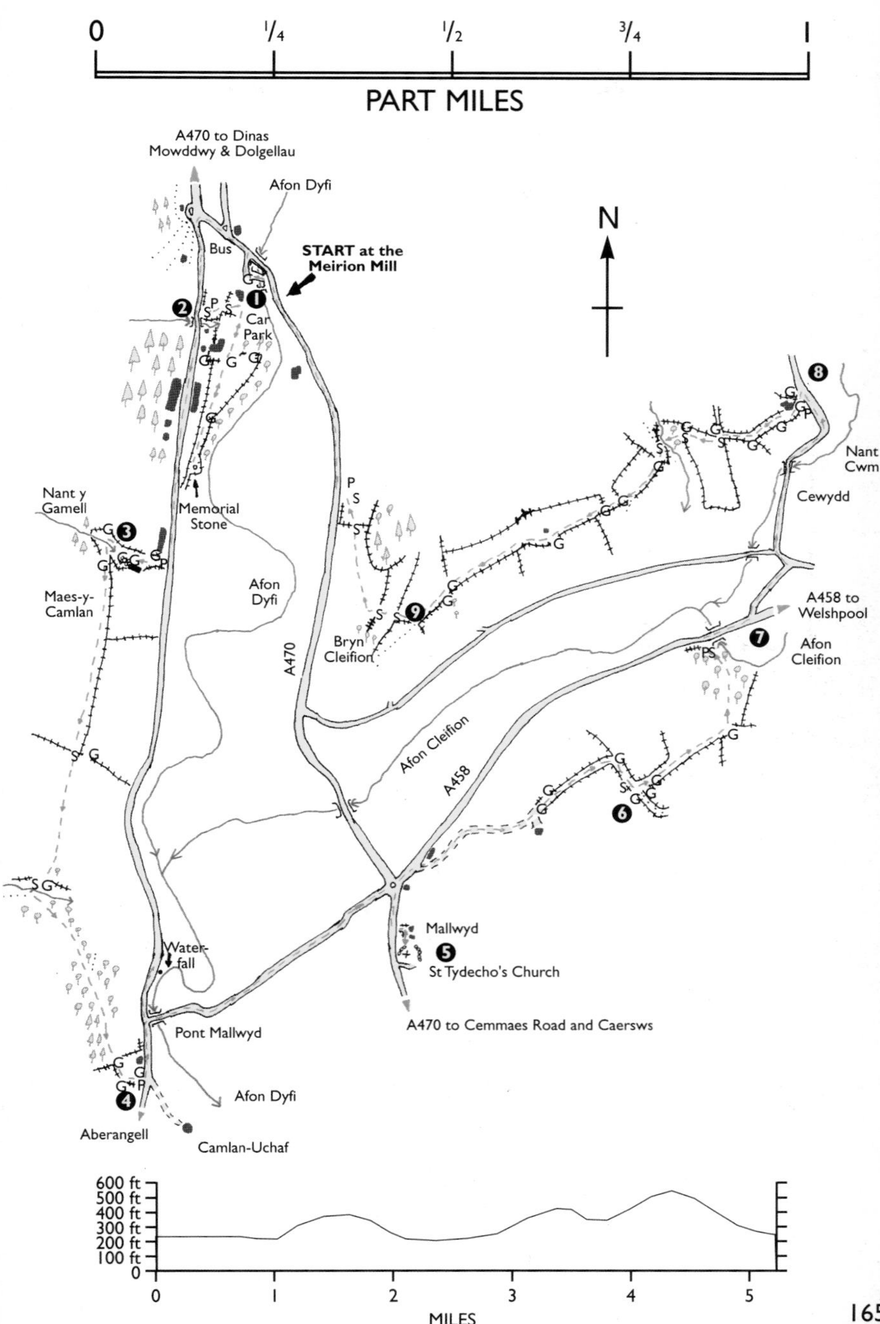

0
1/4
1/2
3/4
1
PART MILES
A470 to Dinas Mowddwy & Dolgellau
Afon Dyfi
N
START at the Meirion Mill
Bus
Car Park
Memorial Stone
Nant y Gamell
Maes-y-Camlan
Afon Dyfi
A470
Bryn Cleifion
Nant Cwm
Cewydd
A458 to Welshpool
Afon Cleifion
Afon Cleifion
A458
Mallwyd
St Tydecho's Church
Waterfall
Pont Mallwyd
A470 to Cemmaes Road and Caersws
Afon Dyfi
Aberangell
Camlan-Uchaf
600 ft
500 ft
400 ft
300 ft
200 ft
100 ft
0
0
1
2
3
4
5
MILES

probably the old Roman road (from Wroxeter to Brithdir). Just before this enclosed track bears right, turn left across a ladder stile and turn right immediately along the top of the pasture. Cross a stile into woodland and emerge across a stream and over another ladder stile. Climb to the old Roman road and go left with it through four gates, keeping the hedge on your left.

9. Don't go through the fifth gateway (there isn't a gate). Turn right up to a stile and go ahead over the brow of the hill (Bryn Cleifion) to gain a view over the battlefield of Camlan. Cross a stile and bear right to another stile halfway up the fence ahead. Continue to descend gradually to a signpost and stile on your left. Go down steps to the A470 and go right along its verge to the bridge across the River Dyfi. Take the older bridge, now closed to traffic, (not the oldest, preserved, packhorse bridge) on your left to return to the entrance of the Meirion Mill.

Overlooking Bardsey 19

Bardsey has been identified as the Isle of Avalon or Afallach, which lay in the west, in the direction of Ireland. Avalon refers to apples, and Geoffrey of Monmouth wrote that Myrddin (Merlin) and Taliesin took the grievously wounded Arthur to the Island of Apples after the Battle of Camlan, where Morgan and her ladies nursed him back to health.

Bardsey is either a Viking or Saxon name, while the Welsh name for the island (Enlli) probably refers to the strong current surrounding it, or perhaps to a local ruler called Fenlli. There was a prince named Afallach in this area during Arthurian times and Modron was named as his daughter. According to the Welsh Triads, she married Urien of Gorre, whom Morgan Le Fay married in Sir Thomas Malory's Le Morte D'Arthur. Modron is Matriona, the Mother Goddess.

Myrddin (Merlin) is said to lie buried on Bardsey, guarding the thirteen treasures of Britain, being Arthur's Cloak of Invisibility, the Sword of Rhydderch Hael, the Hamper of Gwyddno Garanhir, the Horn of Brangaled, the Chariot of Morgan, the Whetstone of Tudwal Tydglyd, the Cloak of Padarn, the Cauldron of Dyrnwch, the Plate of Rhydderch, the Chessboard of Gwenddolau, the Ring of Eluned, the Knife of Llawfrodedd and the Halter of Clyno Eiddyn.

Leys or spirit paths converge on the tip of the Lleyn Peninsula, bringing the souls of the dead towards Bardsey. Perhaps this is why 20,000 saints are said to be buried there, although 900 Christians did flee there in 607 when Ethelfrid, King of Bernicia, destroyed the monastery at Bangor-is-y-Coed (Clwyd). Bardsey became a popular destination for pilgrims, with three pilgrimages there being the equal of one to Rome. The pilgrims used to go down the steps to St. Mary's Well, then pray at St. Mary's Chapel. It is considered lucky to fill your mouth with water from the well and retain it there whilst running three times around the old chapel, making a wish.

All that remains of the chapel today is a grassy mound within an enclosure.

If you want to visit Bardsey - and perhaps stay there - telephone the Observatory Booking Secretary, c/o The Bardsey Trust on 01626 773908.

No. 72 Bardsey Island as seen from St Mary's Well

Overlooking Bardsey

No. 73 Pathway to St Marys Well

Distance: 1 3/4 miles

Grid Reference: SH 140259

Maps: O.S. Pathfinder 843 (Abersoch & Aberdaron), O.S. Landranger 123 (Lleyn Peninsula).

Parking: There is a car park at the start of this walk, near the Coast Guard Lookout on Mynydd Mawr.

Public Transport: The nearest bus stop is three miles to the east at Aberdaron (no 17 from Pwllheli). Telephone 01286 679535 for details, also about an infrequent, seasonal service (no 17B) which comes from Pwllheli and serves Uwchmynydd.

Refreshments: None along this route, but available in Aberdaron.

Start: There is a car park at the top of Mynydd Mawr, at the end of a road which serves the Coastguard look-out. (G.R. SH 140259)

Route

1. Face Bardsey Island (Ynys Enlli) across the Sound. Take a concrete path down towards the sea, stopping at an old gun emplacement. Descend another 100 yards, to a grassy shelf.

2. Turn left to walk above the sea on your right. Descend towards the headland of Trwyn Maen Melyn (Yellowstone Point). There is a distinctive stone covered with yellow moss and pointing out to sea.

3. Continue with the sea on your right to a narrow path which bears right down towards the sea. Steps were cut into the rock many years ago to give access to St. Mary's Well. This is revealed at low tide as a remarkable spring of fresh water, rather overgrown with green weed. Climb inland to pass the site of St. Mary's Chapel and walk with a stream on your right. The National Trust has fenced off part of the land on the far side of this stream as an experiment to compare with the grazed pasture. Go ahead to be joined by a fence on your right, accompanying you to the road.

4. Go left uphill along the road to return to the car park.

The route map for Walk 19 - Overlooking Bardsey

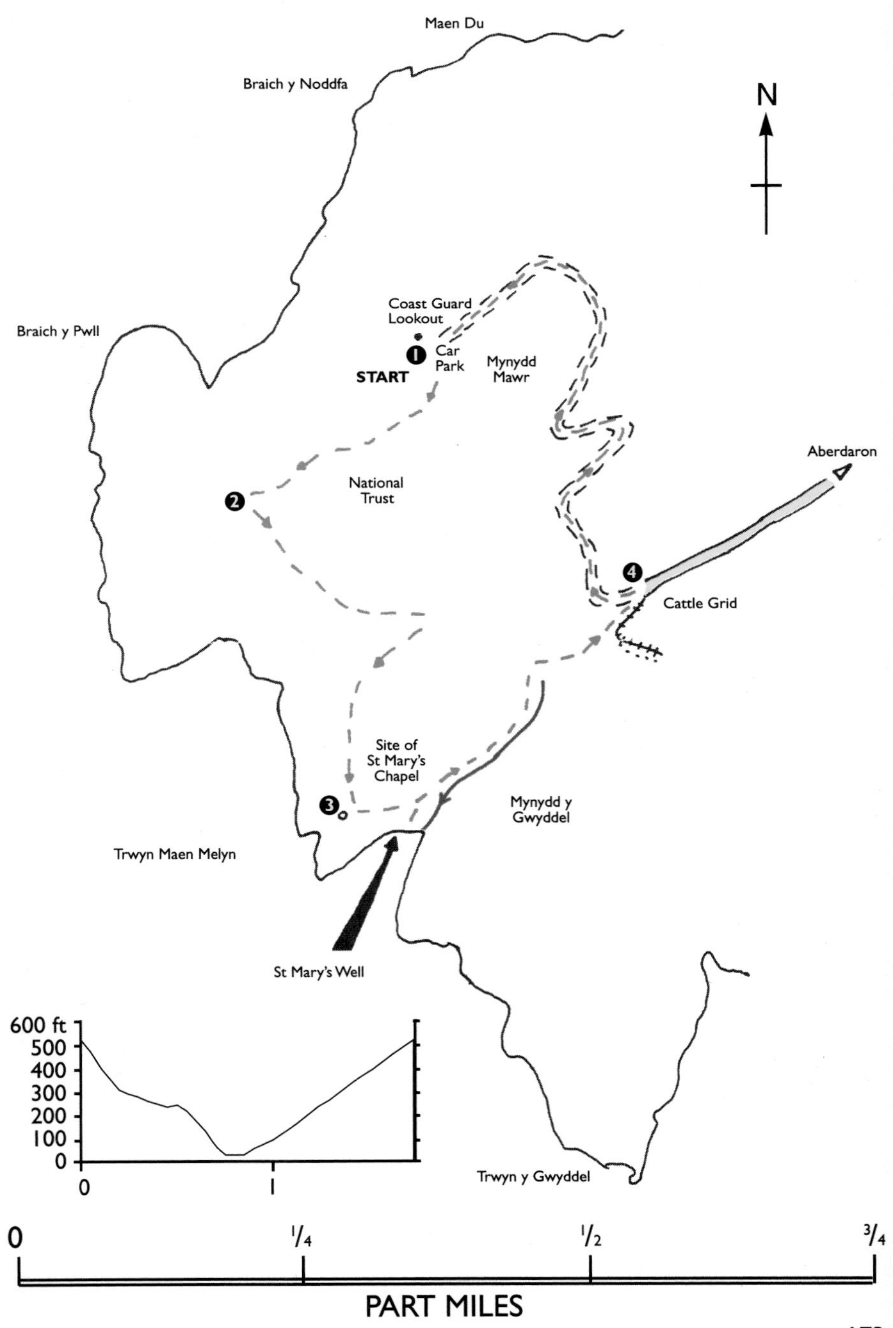

No. 74 Bardsey Island as seen from the coastguard

Craig-y-Ddinas 20

The steep, rugged rock of Craig-y-Ddinas is a favourite haunt of the fairies. This is where the sleeping Arthur is said to wait, along with his knights, for the day they must return. Perhaps they reside in the Celtic underworld of Annwn. The hero sleeping in a cave is an archetype found in dreams gained when sleeping at such spots. The traditional story tells of a Welshman crossing London Bridge, carrying a hazel stick. A stranger noticed the stick and advised him to return to the place he cut it from and dig for buried treasure. Obeying instructions, he dug to find a stone which was raised to reveal a passage (a common feature of dreams at sacred sites where the dreamer is led to Annwn). At the end of the passage was a door, giving admission to a cave. This cave was full of sleeping warriors, with King Arthur sleeping on a throne. The intruder scooped up gold from the floor of the cave without waking its occupants, then he rang a bell. A great voice asked who had rung it and whether the day had come. King Arthur had to be reassured that the day had not come before he and his knights returned to their long sleep. Later, the greedy thief was beaten by Arthur's knights when he made a repeat visit to the cave for more gold. King Arthur's day will come, perhaps sooner than we think.

Craig-y-Ddinas

No. 75 Graig-y-Dinas

Distance:	6 miles
Grid Reference:	SN 947089
Maps:	O.S. Pathfinder 1108 (Hirwaun), O.S. Outdoor Leisure 11 (Brecon Beacons - Central area), O.S. Landranger 160 (Brecon Beacons).
Parking:	Patrons may park at the Lamb Inn, Penderyn, or there is roadside parking nearby.
Public Transport:	Shamrock Buses operate from Pontypridd to Penderyn. Telephone 01222 820626 for details.
Refreshments:	The Lamb Inn and the Red Lion, Penderyn.

Start: Lamb Inn, Penderyn. (G.R. SN 947089)

Route

1. Face the Lamb Inn and go right, soon forking left along the route of an old tramway. A few sleepers survive near the T-junction where a signpost points you ahead along a fenced track which soon bears slightly right.

2. Go ahead through the waymarked gate and keep straight ahead when a path forks right, descending with the fence which was on your right. Pass an old quarry on your left and bear right to cross a stream and ascend.

3. Go ahead across a stile, continue with a fence on your left and ignore a stile in it. Cross a stile beside a gate ahead and turn right to walk the waymarked "permitted footpath/advised path to waterfalls" beside a fence on your right. Reach a signpost near large boulders and turn right down steps to the waterfall Sgwd yr Eira.

4. Climb back up the steps from the waterfall to the signpost at the path junction. Turn right to resume your previous direction, keeping above the steep, wooded slopes of the valley on your right. Follow the waymarked path as it turns right, then left, passing conifer trees. Cross a stream and pass the ruins of Cilhepste-cerig.

5. Continue over a footbridge across another stream and follow the path to a small metal gate. Go through it and pass a signposted path to the Gunpowder Works. Fork left at the next signpost to reach a path junction where the signpost indicates that you keep right to Dinas Rock (Craig-y-Ddinas). Overlook the Sychryd Gorge on your left and the valley of the Afon Mellte on your right.

6. Retrace your steps to the path junction and go ahead along the track signposted as being for Penderyn. Keep to this track, ignoring a path on your right

No. 76 Pathway behind Sgwd-yr-Eira waterfall

down to the Silica Mines. Walk uphill with a wall on your right, continue through two gates, then with a fence on your left to reach a road at a corner.

7. Go ahead down the road to bear left past St Cynog's Church on your left and the Red Lion Inn (Tafarn Llew Goch) on your right. Take the next turning on your right to return to the Lamb Inn, Penderyn.

The route map for Walk 20 - Craig-Y-Ddinas

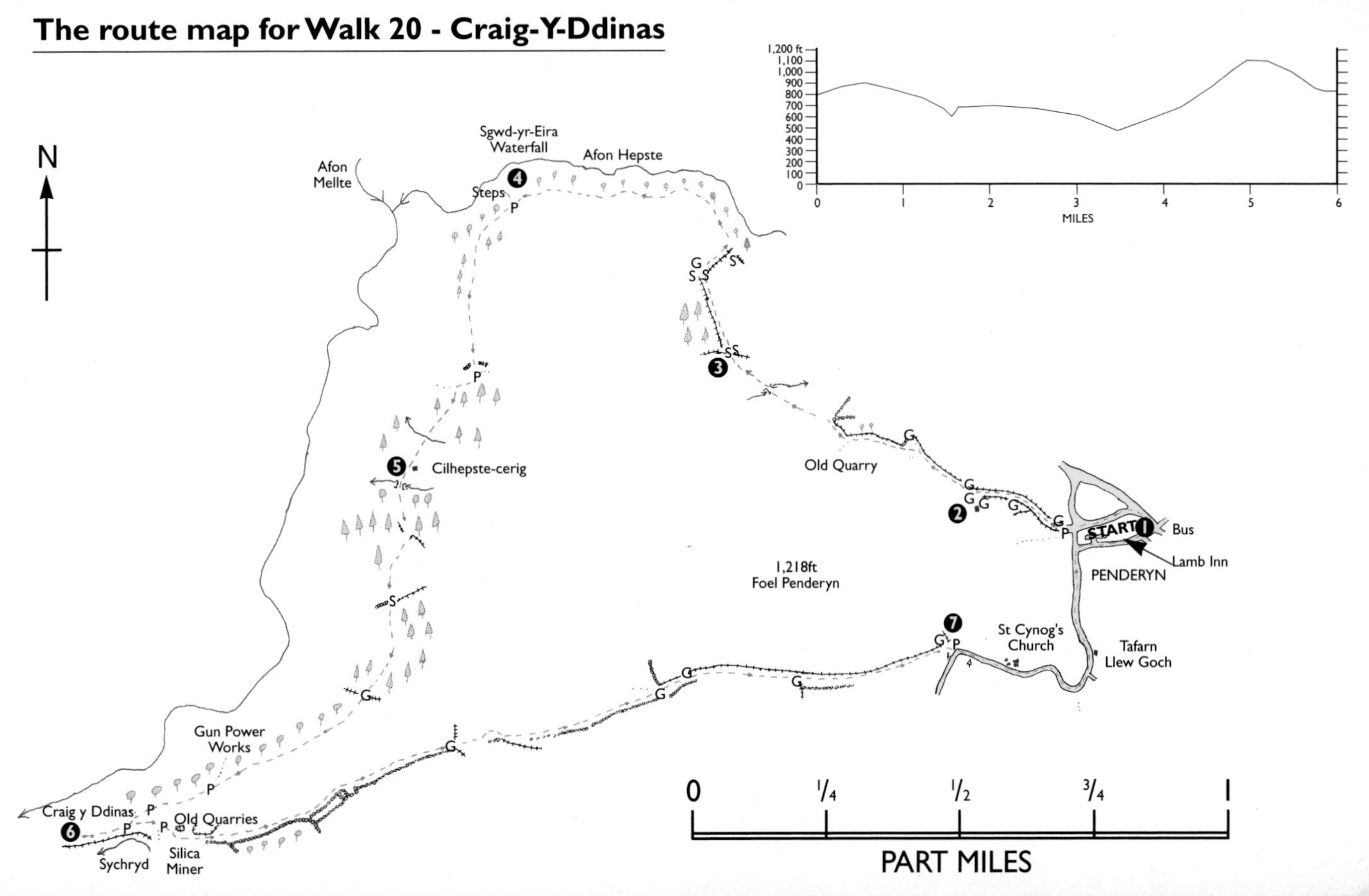

No. 77 Sgwd-yr-Eira Falls

No. 78 Castell Dinas Bran

Walk Notes

Walk Notes

Walk Notes

Walk Notes

No. 80 Cilgerran

Book Publishing Team

Designer - Bev Mitchell

Beverley decided to return to education, becoming a student of design, eight years after leaving school.
In June 1995 she completed foundation studies in art and design at the Cardiff Institute of Higher Education - gaining a distinction.
Previous design commissions include a painting on glass in the Chapel of St. Luke at the University Hospital of Wales, Cardiff.
Beverley was born in 1966 and lives in Llandaff, Cardiff.

Photographer - Phil Martin

Phil Martin first started taking photographs in 1986 when he decided to use the camera to record the rapidly-changing landscape of the Cardiff bay area.
He is now in the third year of a BA (Hons) course in film and photography at Gwent College of higher Education.
His work has been shown at exhibitions in South Wales and Mexico, and in 1994 he won the Allan Jacobs Memorial Award for the best newcomer at the Ffotogallery Ffotoannual exhibition in Cardiff.

Born in 1957, he lives in Cardiff

Illustrator - Jennifer Coles

Jennifer Coles is a professional typesetter and illustrator. Her previous work includes illustrations for a guide to walks on the Glamorgan Heritage Coast.

Born in 1966, she lives in the hamlet of Castellau, near Llantrisant.

Louise Baker, Andrew Jones and Carol Williams are Apple Macintosh Designers who mainly produce magazines and books. They work closely with the designer, illustrator and sometimes author of a book to develop and produce the finished product to film ready for the printers. They are responsible for all typographical and pictorial design, scanning and manipulation of all images.

Graphic Designers/Typesetters - Louise Baker, Andrew Jones, Carol Williams

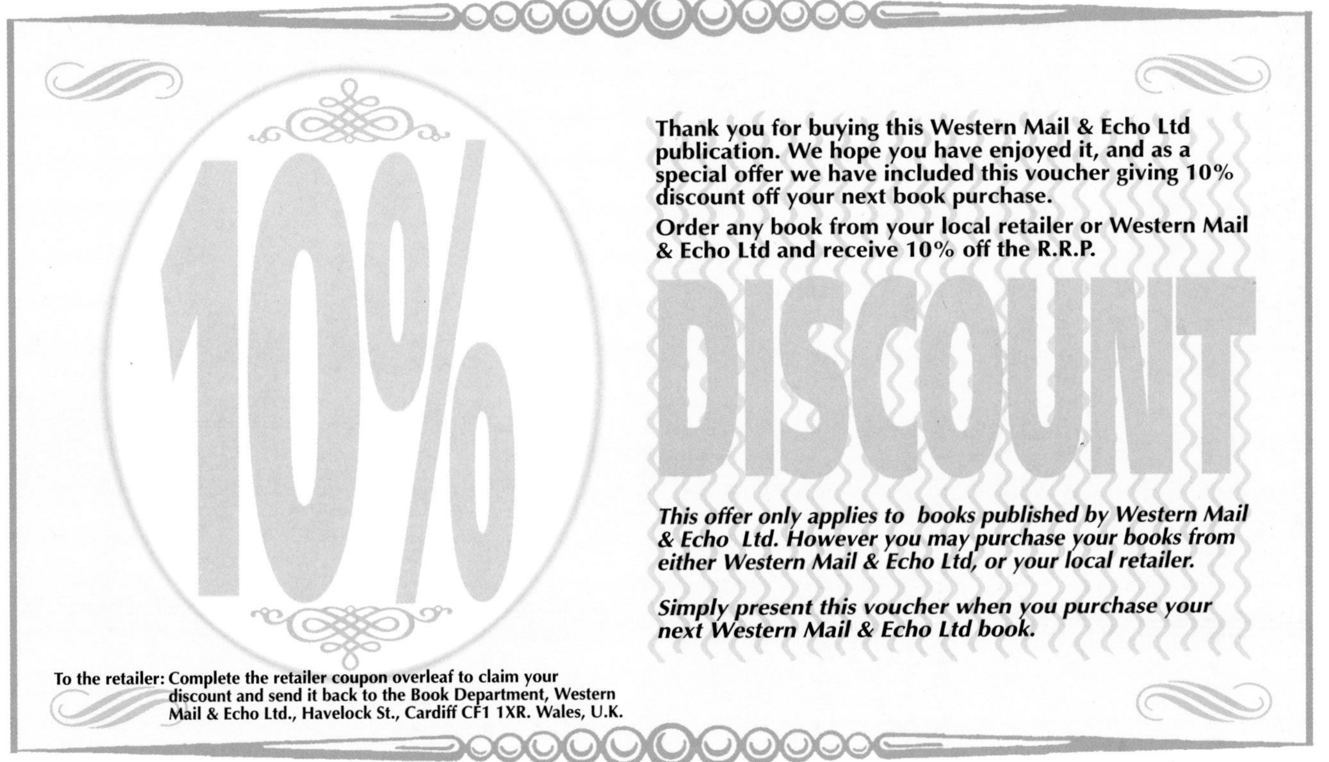
10%
Thank you for buying this Western Mail & Echo Ltd publication. We hope you have enjoyed it, and as a special offer we have included this voucher giving 10% discount off your next book purchase.
Order any book from your local retailer or Western Mail & Echo Ltd and receive 10% off the R.R.P.
DISCOUNT
This offer only applies to books published by Western Mail & Echo Ltd. However you may purchase your books from either Western Mail & Echo Ltd, or your local retailer.
Simply present this voucher when you purchase your next Western Mail & Echo Ltd book.
To the retailer: Complete the retailer coupon overleaf to claim your discount and send it back to the Book Department, Western Mail & Echo Ltd., Havelock St., Cardiff CF1 1XR. Wales, U.K.

RETAILER REDEMPTION COUPON

To the Retailer: Please accept this voucher as 10% discount off the R.R.P. of any Western Mail & Echo Ltd book. For a full refund of this 10% discount, please send this completed coupon to:
The Book Department, Western Mail & Echo Ltd., Thomson House, Havelock Street, Cardiff, CF1 1XR.

When redeeming vouchers please ensure that all the details are completed. Only fully completed coupons are valid. No photocopies.

Retailer details

Name ....

Address ....

....

Town ....

Post Code ....

Tel No. (daytime) ....

Contact name ....

Purchaser/Customer details

Name ....

Address ....

....

Town ....

Post Code ....

Tel No. (daytime) ....

Book title purchased ....

R.R.P. ....

Discount given ....

POSTAL BOOK ORDER FORM ONLY

Order your next books by post for a 10% discount. This only applies to additional purchases.

To: **THE BOOK DEPARTMENT WESTERN MAIL & ECHO Ltd.**
HAVELOCK STREET CARDIFF CF1 1XR WALES

Please rush me the following books to:
(Please print names and address CLEARLY)

Name ....

Address ....

....

Postcode .... Tel: ....

BOOK TITLE	ISBN No	Qty	Price	Total
Gren's Diary 1996	09504042 5X		£5.95	
Gren's Diary 1997 Available Oct 96*	09504042 76		£5.95	
Gren's Guide To Rugby	09504042 68		£4.95	
Images of Cardiff	18598302 85		£12.99	
In the Footsteps of King Arthur	09504042 41		£7.95	
Total quantity/cost				
Special Discount Less 10 %				
Add Postage & Packing @ £3 per book				
Total remmitance enclosed				

Please debit my credit card
(enter card number here) □□□□ □□□□ □□□□ □□□□
(expiry date) □□/□□

Name: .... Signature: ....
(CAPITALS)

Please allow 28 days for delivery on U.K. addresses or call into The Western Mail & Echo Offices in Cardiff, alternatively to purchase one of our books visit your local retailer.

Please note! Post and package applies to U.K. orders only, for overseas P&P add £10 per item.

PHOTOGRAPH ORDER FORM

PHOTOSALES DEPARTMENT
Western Mail & Echo Ltd.,
Thomson House,
Havelock Street,
Cardiff CF1 1XR.
Telephone: 01222 583583

Please send me copies of the following photographs:

Photo Ref N°	Caption reference BLOCK CAPITALS PLEASE	Quantity Size Approx. 8 x 6 ins 20 x 15 cms £8.00 each	Quantity Size Approx 10 x 8 ins 25 x 20 cms £10.00 each	Amount £
No. 77	Sgwd-yr-Eira Falls	1		£8.00
Orders can be collected from The Western Mail & Echo at Thomson House or add post & packing - included to the UK - add £1.00 for overseas only. *(Please allow 28 days for delivery in the UK)*				

Your name & address

Name

Company Name

Address

Town

Post Code

Tel

Delivery address if different

Name

Company name

Address:

Town

Post Code

Tel No

If you wish to pay by credit card enter your number here:

☐☐☐☐ ☐☐☐☐ ☐☐☐☐ ☐☐☐☐

(expiry date) ☐☐/☐☐

Name: ....

(CAPITALS)

Signature: ....

(PLEASE SIGN & SEND TO ABOVE ADDRESS)

WESTERN MAIL & ECHO LTD

PHOTOSALES

ILLUSTRATION ORDER FORM

PHOTOSALES DEPARTMENT

Western Mail & Echo Ltd.,
Thomson House, Havelock Street,
Cardiff CF1 1XR.
Telephone: 01222 583583

We are pleased to offer you copies of ***Jennifer Coles*** *artwork, as seen within the pages of In the* ***Footsteps of King Arthur.*** *The offer only applies to the twenty large drawings supporting the legends.*

Size A4 (approx. 21 x 29 cms / 8 x 11 ins) printed on 160gsm matt art paper. Copy unframed.

Chapter no.	Chapter Title	Description of illustration	Quantity @ £8.00 each	Amount £
e.g.	Dinas Emrys	Dragons	1	£8.00
Postage & packing included to UK only. For overseas orders add £1.00. Alternatively orders can be collected from the Western Mail & Echo Ltd. at Thomson House. *(Please allow 28 days for delivery in the UK)*				
GRAND TOTAL *Please enclose your remittence and make cheques payable to Western Mail & Echo Ltd*				

Your name & address	Delivery address if different
Name	Name
Company Name	Company name
Address	Address:
Town	Town
Post Code	Post Code
Tel	Tel No

If you wish to pay by credit card enter your number here:

□□□□ □□□□ □□□□ □□□□

expiry date) □□/□□

Card Name: ....

(PLEASE PRINT)

Signature: ....

(PLEASE SIGN & SEND TO ABOVE ADDRESS)

WESTERN MAIL & ECHO LTD

PHOTOSALES

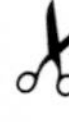